Grace
Abounding

Happy Birthday

"Veronica"

CON AMOR, Tu mamá
ana maria Tacalo

2·14·2015

Editorial assistance by Jill Jones.

Print ISBN 978-1-62029-794-0

eBook Editions:
Adobe Digital Edition (.epub) 978-1-62416-070-7
Kindle and MobiPocket Edition (.prc) 978-1-62416-069-1

Cover image © Corbis Photography

Published by Barbour Publishing, Inc., P.O. Box 719, Uhrichsville, Ohio 44683, www.barbourbooks.com

Our mission is to publish and distribute inspirational products offering exceptional value and biblical encouragement to the masses.

Member of the
Evangelical Christian
Publishers Association

Printed in the United States of America.

Grace
Abounding

ABRIDGED & UPDATED

JOHN
BUNYAN

BARBOUR
PUBLISHING

CONTENTS

INTRODUCTION

Written more than four centuries ago, John Bunyan's *Grace Abounding to the Chief of Sinners* is a Christian classic that still speaks to readers—addressing concerns that trouble the human heart today just as they did in the 1600s.

Grace Abounding gives an account of God's exceeding goodness in the life of "his poor servant John Bunyan"—as well as Bunyan's call to the ministry and his imprisonment for that ministry.

John Bunyan's encounter with God transformed a poorly educated, blaspheming tinker into a bold preacher of the Gospel. As a Christian, Bunyan would also display a genius for writing, authoring more than sixty books, including the classic *Pilgrim's Progress*.

Born at Elstow, Bedfordshire, England, in 1628, Bunyan attended school briefly, followed his father's vocation of repairing household utensils, and served in the parliamentary army during the English civil war.

He then married a woman (whose name has been lost to history) who encouraged him to attend church, where he heard the Gospel. After a long internal struggle, Bunyan surrendered himself to Christ—then embarked on a life of wholehearted commitment to God. He died in 1688, having contracted a fever on a forty-mile horseback ride to preach in London.

The book that follows is a lightly updated version of Bunyan's *Grace Abounding*. It has also been abridged to approximately 80 percent of the length of the original. Please note that when a paragraph number is lacking, it has been removed in the interest of manuscript length and relevance to today's reader.

PREFACE

*A Brief Account of the Publishing of This Work,
Written by the Author and Dedicated to Those
Whom God Has Counted Him Worthy to Lead
to Faith, by His Ministry in the Word*

CHILDREN, grace be with you, amen.
Having been taken from you and so tied up
that I cannot perform my God-given duty
toward you for your edification and building
up in faith and holiness, yet in order that
you may see that my soul has fatherly care
for your spiritual and everlasting welfare, I
now once again, as before from the top of
Shenir and Hermon, so now from the lions'
dens, from the mountains of the leopards
(Song of Solomon 4:8), still look after you
all, greatly longing to see your safe arrival
into the desired haven.

I thank God every time I remember you,
and I rejoice, even while I am stuck between
the teeth of the lions in the wilderness,
at the grace and mercy and knowledge of
Christ our Savior, which God has bestowed
on you, with abundance of faith and love.

Your hunger and thirst also after further acquaintance with the Father in His Son; your tenderness of heart; your trembling at sin; your sober and holy conduct before both God and men are great refreshment to me, "for you are [my] glory and joy" (1 Thessalonians 2:20).

I have enclosed a drop of that honey that I have taken out of the carcass of a lion (Judges 14:5-9). I have eaten of it myself and am much refreshed thereby. (Temptations, when we meet them at first, are as the lion that roared at Samson; but if we overcome them, the next time we see them, we shall find a nest of honey within them.) The Philistines do not understand me. This is something of a relation of the work of God on my own soul, even from the very first till now, in which you will see the times I have been cast down and risen back up. For "He wounds, but His hands make whole" (Job 5:18). It is written in scripture, "The father shall make known Your truth to the children" (Isaiah 38:19). Yes, it was for this reason I stayed so long at Sinai (Deuteronomy 4:10–11), to see the fire and

the cloud and the darkness, that I might
fear the Lord all the days of my life on earth,
and tell of His wondrous works to my
children (Psalm 78:3–5).

Moses (Numbers 33:1–2) wrote of the
journeys of the children of Israel from Egypt
to the land of Canaan, and commanded also
that they remember their forty years' travel
in the wilderness. "And you shall remember
that the LORD your God led you all the
way these forty years in the wilderness, to
humble you and test you, to know what
was in your heart, whether you would keep
His commandments or not" (Deuteronomy
8:2). Therefore I have endeavored to do this
and to publish it also in order that, if God
will, others may be reminded of what He
has done for their souls by reading about
His work in me.

It is profitable for Christians to often call
to mind the very beginnings of grace in their
souls. "It is a night of solemn observance to
the LORD for bringing them out of the land
of Egypt. This is that night of the LORD, a
solemn observance for all the children of
Israel throughout their generations" (Exodus

12:42). "O my God," said David, "my soul
is cast down within me; therefore I will
remember You from the land of the Jordan,
and from the heights of Hermon, from the
Hill Mizar" (Psalm 42:6). He remembered
also the lion and the bear when he went
to fight with the giant of Gath (1 Samuel
17:36–37).

It was Paul's custom (Acts 22) when tried
for his life (Acts 24) to tell his judges the
manner of his conversion. He would think of
that day and that hour in which he first met
with grace, for he found it a support. When
God had brought the children of Israel
through the Red Sea, far into the wilderness,
they had to turn back to remember the
drowning of their enemies there (Numbers
14:25). For though they sang His praise
before, yet they soon forgot his works (Psalm
106:11–13).

In this discourse of mine you will see
much of the grace of God toward me. I
thank God I can count it much, for His
grace was greater than my sins and Satan's
temptations, too. I can remember my fears
and doubts and sad months with comfort;

they are as the head of Goliath in my hand. There was nothing to David like Goliath's sword, for the very sight and memory of it preached God's deliverance to him. Oh, the remembrance of my great sins, of my great temptations, and of my great fears of perishing forever! They bring afresh into my mind the memory of my great help, my great support from heaven, and the great grace that God extended to such a wretch as I.

My dear children, call to mind the former days and the years of ancient times; remember also your songs in the night and commune with your own heart (Psalm 77:5–12). Indeed, look diligently and leave no corner unsearched, for there is treasure hidden, even the treasure of your first and second experience of the grace of God toward you. Remember, I say, the word that first laid hold upon you; remember your terrors of conscience and fear of death and hell; remember also your tears and prayers to God, indeed, how you sighed under every hedge for mercy. Have you a hill Mizar to remember? Have you forgotten the place where God visited your soul? Remember also the Word—the Word, I say, on which the Lord has caused you to hope. If you have sinned against light, if you are tempted to blaspheme, if you are down in despair, if you think God fights against you or if heaven is hidden from your eyes, remember it was thus with your father, but out of them all the Lord delivered me.

I could have expounded much in this discourse on my temptations and troubles with sin, as well as the merciful kindness and working of God in my soul. I could also have used a style much more sophisticated than the one in which I have here discourse and could have adorned my words more than I have seemed to do here, but I dare not. God did not play in convincing me; the devil did not play in tempting me; neither did I play when I sank as into a bottomless pit, when the pangs of hell caught hold of me. Therefore I may not play in my relating of them but must be plain and simple and lay down the account as it happened. He who likes it, let him receive it; and he who does not, let him produce a better. Farewell.

My dear children, the milk and honey

are beyond this wilderness. God be merciful to you and grant that you not be slothful to go in to possess the land.

GRACE ABOUNDING TO
THE CHIEF OF SINNERS

A Brief Relation of the Exceeding Mercy of God in Christ, to His Poor Servant John Bunyan

1. In relating the merciful working of God on my soul, it would not be out of order for me to start by giving you, in a few words, a hint of my pedigree and upbringing, that the goodness and bounty of God toward me may be the more magnified before the sons of men.

2. As for my descent, it was of a low and inconsiderable generation, my father's house being of that rank that is poorest and most despised of all the families in the land. While I cannot boast, as others, of noble blood or of a highborn state according flesh, I magnify the heavenly Majesty this door He brought me into this wo partake of the grace and life that is in by the Gospel.

3. Yet in spite of the lowliness and obscurity of my parents, it pleased God to put it into their hearts to send me to school to learn to read and write, which I did, according to the rate of other poor men's children. To my shame, I confess, I soon lost what little I learned, and that almost utterly, long before the Lord worked His gracious work of conversion upon my soul.

4. As for my own natural life, for the time that I was without God in the world, it was indeed according to the course of this world and the spirit who now works in the sons of disobedience (Ephesians 2:2–3). It was my delight to be taken captive by the devil to do his will (2 Timothy 2:26). I was filled with all unrighteousness, which had so strongly worked and put forth itself in both my heart and life since I was a child that I had equals for cursing, swearing, lying, and blaspheming the holy name of God.

Indeed, so settled and rooted was I in these things that they became second nature to me; these things, as I have with soberness considered since, so offended the Lord that even in my childhood He frightened me with fearful dreams and terrified me with dreadful visions. Often, after I had spent a day in sin, I lay in my bed greatly afflicted as I slept with apprehensions of devils and wicked spirits, who still labored to draw me away with them and of which I could never be rid.

6. During these years I was also greatly afflicted and troubled with thoughts of the day of judgment, both night and day, and trembled at the thought of the fearful torments of hellfire, still fearing that it would be my lot to be found at last among those devils and hellish fiends who are there bound down with the chains and bonds of eternal darkness until the judgment of the great day (Jude 1:6).

7. These things, when I was nine or ten years old, so distressed my soul that when in the midst of my many sports and childish vanities, amidst my vain companions, I was often much afflicted in my mind, yet I could not let go of my sins. Indeed, I was also so overcome with despair of life and heaven that I often wished either that there had been no hell or that I had been a devil— supposing they were only tormentors— and that if I had to go there, I might be a tormentor rather than be tormented myself.

8. Awhile after, these terrible dreams left me and I soon forgot them, for my pleasures quickly cut off the memory of them as if they had never been. With more greediness, according to the strength of nature, I still let loose the reins to my lusts and delighted in all transgression against the law of God, so much so that, until I came to the state of marriage, I was the very ringleader of all the youth that kept me company into all manner of vice and ungodliness.

9. Indeed, such free rein had the lusts and fruits of the flesh in this poor soul of mine that if a miracle of precious grace had not intervened, I would not only have perished by the stroke of eternal justice but would have also laid myself open to the stroke of those laws that bring some to disgrace and open shame before the face of the world.

10. In those days, thoughts of religion were very grievous to me; I could neither endure religion myself nor that any other should. When I read in books about Christian piety, it was like a prison to me. Then I said unto God, "Depart from [me], for [I] do not desire the knowledge of Your ways" (Job 21:14). I was now devoid of all good consideration, heaven and hell were both out of sight and mind, and as for saving and damning, they were least in my thoughts. *O Lord, You know my life, and my ways were not hidden from You.*

11. Yet this I well remember, that though I could myself sin with the greatest delight and ease, and also take pleasure in the vileness of my companions, yet if at any time I saw wicked things being done by those who professed goodness, it made my spirit tremble. When I was in the height of my vanity, if I heard one swear who was reckoned to be a religious man, it made my heart ache.

12. But God did not utterly leave me but followed me still, not with convictions but with judgments, yet such as were mixed with mercy. For once I fell into a creek and hardly escaped drowning. Another time I fell out of a boat into Bedford River, but mercy preserved me. Another time when I was in a field with one of my companions, an adder passed over the highway. Having a stick in my hand, I struck it over the back, and having stunned it, I forced open its mouth with my stick and plucked its fangs out with my fingers. If God had not been merciful, I might have brought myself to my end. . . .

14. Here were judgments and mercy, but neither of them awakened my soul to righteousness. I sinned still and grew more and more rebellious against God and careless of my own salvation.

15. Soon after this, I changed my condition into a married state, and my mercy was to marry a wife whose father was considered godly. This woman and I, though we came together as poor as poor might be, not

having so much household stuff as a dish
or spoon between us both, yet this she had:
The Plain Man's Pathway to Heaven and
The Practice of Piety, which her father had
left her when he died. In these two books
I sometimes read with her, and in them
I found some things that were somewhat
pleasing to me; but all this while I met with
no conviction. She often told me what a
godly man her father was and how he would
reprove and correct vice, both in his house
and among his neighbors, and what a strict
and holy life he lived in his day, both in
word and deed.

16. Though these books did not reach my
heart to awaken it to my sad and sinful state,
yet they awakened within me some desire
for religion, so that, because I knew no
better, I participated eagerly in the religion
of the times. I went to church twice a day
and very devoutly said and sang as others
did, yet I retained my wicked life. But I was
so overrun with a spirit of superstition that
I adored all things—the high place, priest,
clerk, vestment, service, and everything else

belonging to the church, considering all things holy that were therein contained. . . .

19. But all this while I was not sensible of the danger and evil of sin; I was kept from considering that sin would damn me, whatever religion I followed, unless I was found in Christ. I never thought of Him, nor whether He existed. Thus man, while blind, wanders but wearies himself with vanity, for he knows not the way to the city of God (Ecclesiastes 10:15).

20. But one day, our parson preached on how to treat the Sabbath day, and the evil of breaking it with labor, sports, or otherwise. Now I was, despite my religion, one who took much delight in all manner of vice, especially on the Sabbath, so my conscience fell under his sermon, believing that he preached it on purpose to show me my evildoing. At that time I felt guilt as I never had before that I can remember. I was, for the present, greatly burdened with it and went home when the sermon was ended with a great burden on my spirit.

21. For that instant, this made my former pleasures taste bitter to me; but the feeling did not last, for before I had finished dining, the trouble began to leave my mind and my heart returned to its old course. How glad was I that this trouble was gone from me and that the fire was put out, that I might sin again without control! When I had satisfied nature with food, I shook the sermon out of my mind and returned to my old custom of sports and gaming with great delight.

22. But the same day, as I was in the midst of a game, a voice suddenly darted from heaven into my soul. It said, "Will you leave your sins and go to heaven or have your sins and go to hell?" I looked up to heaven and saw, as if I had the eyes of understanding, the Lord Jesus looking down on me, looking very displeased with me, as if He were severely threatening me with some grievous punishment for these and other ungodly practices.

23. Suddenly this conclusion was fastened on my spirit: that I had been a great sinner and that it was now too late for me to look for heaven, for Christ would not pardon my transgressions. While I was thinking about this and fearing that it was so, I felt my heart sink in despair, concluding that it was too late. Therefore I resolved in my mind that I would go on in sin; for, thought I, if the case be thus, my state is surely miserable: miserable if I leave my sins and miserable if I follow them. I can but be damned, and if I must be so, I might as well be damned for many sins as for few.

24. Thus I stood in the midst of my play, before those who were then present, yet I told them nothing. But, having made this conclusion, I returned desperately to my sport, and I well remember that soon this kind of despair so possessed my soul that I was persuaded I could never attain to any other comfort than what I could get from sin, for heaven was gone already, so on that I must not think. Therefore I found within me a great desire to take my fill of sin, that

I might taste the sweetness of it; and I made as much haste as I could to fill my belly with its delicacies, lest I should die before I had achieved my desire, for that I feared greatly.

25. And I am very confident that this temptation of the devil is more common among poor creatures than many are aware of, to overrun their spirits with a seared frame of heart and numb their consciences, while he slyly supplies them with such despair that though not much guilt attends the soul, yet they continually have a secret conclusion within them that there is no hope for them, for they have loved sins, therefore after them they will go (Jeremiah 2:25; 18:12).

26. Now, therefore, I went on in sin with great greediness of mind, still grudging that I could not be as satisfied with it as I wanted. I continued this way about a month or more. But one day, as I was standing at a neighbor's shop window, cursing and swearing and playing the madman, according to my usual manner, inside there sat the woman of the house, who heard me and who, though she was a loose and ungodly wretch, protested that I swore and cursed at such a fearful rate that she trembled to hear me. She told me furthermore that I was the most ungodly fellow for swearing that she had ever heard in all her life, and that I was able to spoil all the youth in a whole town if they came into my presence.

27. At this reproof I was silenced and put to secret shame, and that, too, before the God of heaven. While I stood there, hanging my head, I wished with all my heart that I might be a little child again, that my father might teach me to speak without this wicked way of swearing. *For*, thought I, *I am so accustomed to it that it is in vain for me to think of reforming.*

28. But how this came to pass, I know not: from this time forward I so completely left my swearing that it was a great wonder to myself to observe it. And whereas before I knew not how to speak unless I put an oath before and another behind to make my words have authority, now I could, without swearing, speak better and with more pleasantness than I ever could before. All this while I knew not Jesus Christ and did not leave my sports and plays.

29. But soon after this, I spent time with one poor man who made profession of religion, who, as I then thought, talked pleasantly about the scriptures and matters of religion. Liking what he said, I began to take great pleasure in reading my Bible, but especially the historical parts, for I could not understand Paul's epistles and scriptures of that nature, being as yet ignorant of both the corruption of my nature and the need and worth of Jesus Christ to save me.

30. At this time I experienced some outward reformation, both in my words and life, and set the commandments before me for my way to heaven. These commandments I also strived to keep and, as I thought, kept them pretty well sometimes and thought I should have comfort. Yet now and then I broke one and so afflicted my conscience, but then I would repent and say I was sorry for it and promise God to do better next time. In this way I thought I pleased God as well as any man in England.

31. Thus I continued about a year, during which time our neighbors considered me to be a very godly man, a new and religious man, and marveled much to see such a great and famous alteration in my life and manners. And indeed so it was, though yet I knew not Christ, nor grace, nor faith, nor hope. Truly, as I have well seen since, if I had died then, my state would have been most fearful.

32. But, as I said, my neighbors were amazed at my great conversion, from prodigious profaneness to something like a moral life. They began to praise, to commend, and to speak well of me, both to my face and behind my back. Now I was, as they said, become godly; now I was become a right honest man. But oh! when I understood that these were their words and opinions of me, it pleased me mighty well. For though, as yet, I was nothing but a poor painted hypocrite, yet I loved to be talked of as one who was truly godly. I was proud of my godliness, and I did all I did to either be seen of or to be well spoken of by man. And thus I continued for about a year or more.

33. Now you must know that before this I had taken much delight in bell ringing, but, my conscience beginning to be tender, I thought such practice was vain and therefore forced myself to leave it, yet my mind hankered for it. So I would go to the steeple house and look at it, though I dared not ring. But I thought this was not appropriate for religion either, yet I forced myself and would still look on. But soon I began to think, *What if one of the bells should fall?* Then I chose to stand under a main beam that lay across the steeple, from side to side, thinking there I might stand safely, but then I would think again, *If the bell fell with a swing, it might first hit the wall and then, rebounding upon me, might kill me.* This made me stand in the steeple door.

Now, thought I, *I am safe enough; for if a bell should then fall, I can slip out behind these thick walls and so be preserved.*

34. So, after this, I would still go to see them ring but would not go farther than the steeple door; but then it came into my head, *What if the steeple itself should fall?* And this thought so shook my mind that I dared not stand at the steeple door any longer but was forced to flee, for fear the steeple would fall upon my head.

35. Another thing was my dancing. It was a full year before I could quite leave that; but all this while, when I thought I kept this or that commandment, or did anything that I thought was good, I had great peace in my conscience and would think to myself, *God cannot choose but to be pleased with me now.* Indeed, to relate it in my own way, I thought no man in England could please God better than I.

36. But, poor wretch that I was, I was all this while ignorant of Jesus Christ and setting about to establish my own righteousness. I would have perished therein if God, in mercy, had not shown me more of my state of nature.

37. But one day, the good providence of God sent me to Bedford to work on my calling. In one of the streets of that town, I came where there were three or four poor women sitting at a door in the sun, talking about the things of God. Being now willing to hear them discourse, I drew near to hear what they said, for I was now a brisk talker myself in the matters of religion. But I understood not what they said, for their words were beyond my knowledge. Their talk was about a new birth, the work of God on their hearts, and how they were convinced of their miserable state by nature. They talked about how God had visited their souls with His love in the Lord Jesus and with what words and promises they had been refreshed, comforted, and supported against the temptations of the devil. Moreover, they discussed the suggestions and temptations of Satan in particular and told each other which ones they had been afflicted by and how they were delivered from his assaults. They also spoke of their own wretchedness of heart, of their unbelief, and they scorned, slighted, and abhorred their own righteousness as filthy and insufficient to do them any good.

38. And they spoke as if joy made them speak; they spoke with such pleasantness of scripture language and with such appearance of grace in all they said that they were to me as if they had found a new world, as if they were people that dwelt alone and were not to be reckoned among their neighbors (Numbers 23:9).

39. At this I felt my own heart begin to shake, for I saw that in all my thoughts about religion and salvation, the new birth never entered my mind, neither knew I the comfort of the Word and promise, nor the deceitfulness and treachery of my own wicked heart. As for secret thoughts, I took no notice of them; neither did I understand what Satan's temptations were or how they were to be withstood and resisted.

40. When I had heard and considered
what they said, I left them and went about
my employment again, but their discourse
went with me. My heart wanted to tarry
with them, for I was greatly affected by
their words, both because by them I was
convinced that I wanted the true tokens of a
truly godly man, and also because by them
I was convinced of the happy and blessed
condition of him who was such.

41. Therefore I would often make it
my business to go again and again into
the company of these poor people, for I
could not stay away; and the more I went
among them, the more I questioned my
condition. Presently I found two things
within me, at which I sometimes marveled:
one was a great softness and tenderness
of heart, which caused me to fall under
the conviction of what they asserted by
scripture, and the other was a great bending
in my mind to a continual meditating on
it and on all other good things that at any
time I heard or read of.

42. By these things my mind was now so affected that it lay like a leech at the vein, still crying out, "Give and give!" (Proverbs 30:15). Indeed, it was so fixed on eternity and on the things of the kingdom of heaven, so far as I knew them, that neither pleasures nor profits nor persuasions nor threats could loosen it or make it let go its hold. It would have been as difficult for me to have taken my mind from heaven to earth, as I have often found it since, to get it again from earth to heaven.

43. One thing I may not omit: There was a young man in our town to whom my heart was knit more than to any other, but because he was a most wicked creature for cursing and swearing and whoring, I now forsook his company. But about a quarter of a year after I had left him, I met him and asked how he was doing. He, in his old swearing and mad way, answered that he was well. "But, Harry," said I, "why do you swear and curse thus? What will become of you if you die in this condition?" He answered me hotly, "What would the devil do for company if it were not for such as I am?"

44. About this time I came across some Ranters' [a religious sect of the 1600s] books that were put forth by some of our countrymen and were held in high esteem by several old believers. Some of these I read but was not able to make a judgment about them. As I read them and thought about them, feeling myself unable to judge, I prayed, "O Lord, I am a fool and not able to know the truth from error. Lord, leave me not to my own blindness, either to approve of or to condemn this doctrine; if it be of God, let me not despise it; if it be of the devil, let me not embrace it. Lord, I lay my soul, in this matter, only at Your foot. Let me not be deceived, I humbly beseech You." I had one religious companion all this while, the poor man that I spoke of before, but about this time he turned into a devilish Ranter and gave himself up to all manner of filthiness. He also denied that there was a God, angel, or spirit and laughed at all exhortations to sobriety. When I labored to rebuke his wickedness, he laughed all the more and pretended that he had gone through all religions and had not been able to decide on the right one till now. He told me also that in a little while we would see all believers turning to the ways of the Ranters. Hating those cursed principles, I left his company and became to him as great a stranger as I had been before a familiar.

45. This man was not the only temptation to me; since my calling lay in the country, I happened to come into the company of several people who were also swept away by the Ranters, though they were formerly strict in religion. These would talk with me of their ways and condemn me as legalistic, pretending that they had only attained to perfection and could do what they wanted and not sin. Oh! these temptations were suitable to my flesh, I being but a young man and my nature in its prime; but God, who had, I hope, designed me for better things, kept me in the fear of His name and did not allow me to accept such principles. And blessed be God, He put it into my heart to cry to Him to be kept and directed, as I still did not trust my own wisdom. I have since seen the effect of that prayer, in His preserving me not only from Ranting errors but also from those who have sprung up since. The Bible was precious to me in those days.

46. And now I began to look into the Bible with new eyes and read it as I never had before. The epistles of the apostle Paul were especially sweet and pleasant to me, and, indeed, I was never out of the Bible, either by reading or meditation, and was still crying out to God that I might know the truth and the way to heaven.

47. As I read, I came across this passage: "To one is given the word of wisdom through the Spirit, to another the word of knowledge through the same Spirit, to another faith. . ." (1 Corinthians 12:8–9). And though I have since seen that by this scripture the Holy Spirit intends things extraordinary, yet on me it then fastened with conviction that I wanted things ordinary, even the understanding and wisdom that other Christians had. On this verse I mused and could not tell what to do, especially regarding the word *faith*, for I sometimes had to question whether I had any faith at all, for I feared that it shut me out of all the blessings that other good people had been given. But I was loath to conclude I had no faith in my soul, *for if I do not,* thought I, *then I should count myself a castaway indeed.*

48. *Now,* said I to myself, *though I am convinced that I am an ignorant drunk and want the blessed gifts of knowledge and understanding that other good people have, yet I do not think I am altogether faithless, though I know not what faith is.* For it was shown to me that those who conclude themselves to be in a faithless state have neither rest nor quiet in their souls, and I was loath to fall completely into despair.

49. Therefore, by this suggestion, I was made afraid, for a while, to see my lack of faith, but God would not allow me to thus undo and destroy my soul but continually created within me such suppositions that I could not rest content until I came to some certain knowledge of whether I had faith or not, this always running in my mind: *But what if you want faith indeed? How can you tell if you have faith?* And besides, I saw for certain that if I did not have it, I was sure to perish forever.

50. So though I endeavored at first to look into the business of faith, yet in a little while I was willing to put myself on trial to see whether I had faith or not. But so ignorant was I that I no more knew how to do it than I know how to begin and complete a rare piece of art that I have never seen or considered.

51. While I was considering these things, the tempter came in with the delusion that there was no way for me to know if I had faith but by trying to work some miracle, enforcing his temptation with those scriptures that seem to point that way. One day as I was between Elstow and Bedford, the temptation was hot upon me to see if I had faith by doing some miracle. The miracle at that time was this: I must say to the puddles in the road, "Be dry," and to the dry places, "You be the puddles." And truly one time I was going to say this, but just as I was about to speak, this thought came into my mind: *But go under that hedge over there and pray first that God would make you able.* But when I had decided to pray, this thought came hot upon me: That if I prayed and came again and tried to do it yet nothing happened, then I could be sure I had no faith but was a castaway and lost. *No*, thought I, *if it be so, I will never try but will stay a little longer.*

52. So I continued at a great loss, for I concluded that if only those who can do wonderful things had faith, then I neither had it nor was ever likely to have it. Thus I was tossed between the devil and my own ignorance and so perplexed that I could not tell what to do.

53. About this time the state and happiness of the poor people of Bedford were presented to me in a dream or vision. I saw them sitting on the sunny side of some high mountain, refreshing themselves with the pleasant beams of the sun, while I was shivering and shrinking in the cold, afflicted with frost, snow, and dark clouds. I thought that also, between me and them, I saw a wall that encompassed the mountain. Now, through this wall my soul greatly desired to pass, and I concluded that, if I could, I would go into the very midst of them and there comfort myself also with the heat of their sun.

54. I tried again and again to see if I could find some passage by which I might enter the wall, but none could I find for some time. At last I saw a narrow gap, like a little doorway in the wall, through which I attempted to pass, but the passage being very narrow, I made many efforts to get in, but all in vain, until I was quite beat. At last, with great striving, I got my head through, and after that my shoulders and my whole body. Then I was exceedingly glad and went and sat down in the midst of them and so was comforted with the light and heat of their sun.

55. Now, this mountain and wall, etc., were thus made out to me—the mountain signified the Church of the living God; the sun that shone thereon, the comfortable shining of His merciful face on those who were therein; the wall, I thought, was the Word, which made separation between the Christians and the world; and the gap that was in this wall I thought was Jesus Christ, who is the way to God the Father (John 14:6; Matthew 7:14). But since the passage was narrow, so narrow that I could not enter into it without great difficulty, it showed me that no one could enter into life but those who were in earnest and those who left this wicked world behind them. For here was room only for body and soul, not for body and soul and sin.

56. This vision weighed on my spirit many days, during which time I saw myself in a forlorn condition yet was provoked to a vehement hunger and desire to be one of that number that sat in the sunshine. Now also I prayed wherever I was and often lifted up my heart, singing that verse in the 51st

Psalm, "Have mercy upon me, O God," for as yet I knew not where I was.

57. Neither could I attain to any comfortable persuasion that I had faith in Christ; but instead of having satisfaction, my soul began to be assaulted with fresh doubts about my future happiness, especially with these: Was I one of the elect? But what if the day of grace was already past?

58. By these two questions I was very much afflicted, sometimes by one and sometimes by the other. In regard to my questioning my election, I found at this time that though I was on fire to find the way to heaven and glory, yet this question so discouraged me that sometimes it was as if the very strength of my body had been taken away. This scripture also seemed to me to trample on all my desires: "It is not of him who wills, nor of him who runs, but of God who shows mercy" (Romans 9:16).

59. With this scripture I could not tell what to do, for I saw that unless God had voluntarily chosen me to be a vessel of mercy, no good could come of my longing and laboring for it. Therefore, this thought still stuck with me: *How can you tell that you are one of the elect? And what if you are not? What then?*

60. *O Lord*, thought I, *what if I am not indeed?* "It may be you are not," said the tempter. *It may be so indeed*, thought I. "Why then," said Satan, "you might as well strive no further, for if you are not chosen of God, there is no talk of your being saved; for it is not of him who wills, nor of him who runs, but of God who shows mercy."

61. By these things I was driven to my wits' end. I hardly thought that Satan was assaulting me but rather that it was my own prudence to start the question. For I heartily agreed that only the elect attained eternal life, but whether I myself was one of them, there lay the question.

62. For several days I was greatly assaulted and perplexed and was often, when I was walking, ready to sink, being faint in my mind. But one day, as I was about ready to give up all hope of ever attaining life, this sentence fell upon my spirit: "Look at the generations of old. Did ever any trust in the Lord and get confounded?" (See Psalm 22:5.)

63. At this thought I was greatly encouraged, for at that very instant it was expounded to me: Begin at the beginning of Genesis and read to the end of the Revelation, and see if you can find if there were ever any who trusted in the Lord who were confounded. So, coming home, I went to my Bible to see if I could find that saying, not doubting that I would find it presently, for it was so fresh and gave my spirit such strength and comfort that it was as if it talked with me.

64. Well, I looked, but I found it not, only it stuck with me. Then I asked first one good man and then another if they knew where it was, but they knew no such place. At this I wondered that such a sentence should so suddenly and with such comfort and strength seize upon and abide in my heart, and yet no one could find it, for I doubted not that it was in the holy scriptures.

65. Thus I continued over a year and could not find the place, but at last, looking into the Apocrypha books, I found it in Ecclesiasticus 2:10. This, at first, somewhat daunted me, but because I had gotten more experience by this time of the love and kindness of God, it troubled me less, especially when I considered that though it was not in those texts that we call holy and canonical, yet because this sentence was the sum and substance of many of the promises, it was my duty to take the comfort it offered. I bless God for that word, for it was of God to me. That word still, at times, shines before my face.

66. After this, that other doubt came on me with strength: *But what if the day of grace is already past? What if you have passed the time of mercy?* Now, I remember that one day, as I was walking into the country, I was thinking much about this, and to aggravate my

trouble, the tempter presented to my mind
the good people of Bedford and suggested to
me that since they were converted already,
they were all that God would save in those
parts and that I came too late, for they had
gotten the blessing before I came.

67. Now was I in great distress, thinking
that this might well be so. I went up
and down bemoaning my sad condition,
counting myself far worse than a thousand
fools for putting off salvation this long and
spending so many years in sin as I had done.
I cried out, "Oh, that I had turned sooner!
Oh, that I had turned seven years ago!" It
made me also angry with myself to think
that I should have nothing to do but trifle
away my time till my soul and heaven were
lost.

68. But when I had been long vexed with
this fear and was scarcely able to take
another step, just about the same place
where I received my other encouragement,
these words broke in upon my mind:
"Compel them to come in, that my house

may be filled"; for yet there is room (Luke 14:22–23). These words, but especially "for yet there is room," were sweet to me, for truly I saw by them that there was room in heaven for me. And moreover, when the Lord Jesus spoke these words, He thought of me, and He, knowing that the time would come when I would be afflicted with fear that there was no place left for me in His bosom, spoke this word and left it on record that I might find help against this vile temptation. This I truly believed.

69. In the light and encouragement of this word I went awhile, and the comfort was greater when I thought that the Lord Jesus thought of me so long ago and that He spoke those words on purpose for my sake to encourage me.

70. But I was not without temptations to go back again; temptations, I say, from Satan, my own heart, and carnal friends. But I thank God these were outweighed by that sound sense of death and of the day of judgment that stayed with me continually. I would often also think of Nebuchadnezzar, of whom it is said, "Because of the majesty that He gave him, all peoples, nations, and languages trembled and feared before him" (Daniel 5:19). Yet I thought, if this great man had all his portion in this world, one hour in hellfire would make him forget everything. This consideration was a great help to me.

71. About this time, I was almost made to see something concerning the beasts that Moses counted clean and unclean. I thought those beasts were types of men—the clean were the people of God, but the unclean were the children of the wicked one. Now, I read that the clean beasts chewed the cud; that is, thought I, they show us we must feed upon the Word of God. They also parted the hoof. I thought that signified we must part, if we would be saved, with the ways of ungodly men. And also, in further reading about them, I found that though we chewed the cud as the hare, yet if we walked with claws like a dog or if we parted the hoof like the swine, yet if we did not chew the cud

as the sheep, we were still unclean. For I
thought the hare to be a type of those who
talk of the Word yet walk in the ways of sin,
and that the swine was like him who parted
with his outward pollutions but still lacked
the Word of faith, without which there
could be no way of salvation, no matter
how devout a man was (Deuteronomy 14).
After this I found, by reading the Word,
that those who must be glorified with Christ
in another world must be called by Him
here—called to the partaking of a share in
His Word and righteousness, to the comforts
and firstfruits of His Spirit, and to a peculiar
interest in all those heavenly things that
prepare the soul for that rest and house of
glory that is in heaven above.

72. Here, again, I was at a standstill, not
knowing what to do, fearing I was not
called. *For*, thought I, *if I am not called, what
then can do me good?* Only those who are
called inherit the kingdom of heaven. But
oh! how I now loved those words that spoke
of a Christian's calling, as when the Lord
said to one, "Follow Me," and to another,

"Come after Me." *And oh!* thought I, *if He would say so to me, too, how gladly would I run after Him!*

73. I cannot now express with what longings and brokenness in my soul I cried to Christ to call me. Thus I continued for a time, on fire to be converted to Jesus Christ, and I also saw that day such glory in a converted state that I could not be content without a share therein. Gold! If I could have gotten it for gold, what would I have given for it! If I had a whole world, it would all have gone ten thousand times over so that my soul might be converted.

74. How lovely now was everyone in my eyes that I thought to be converted men and women! They shone, they walked like people who carried the broad seal of heaven about them. Oh! I saw that the lines had fallen to them in pleasant places, and they had a good inheritance (Psalm 16:6). But what made me sick was that Christ, in Mark, went up into a mountain and called to Him those whom He chose, and they came to Him (Mark 3:13).

75. This scripture made me faint and fearful, yet it kindled fire in my soul. What made me fear was that Christ would have no desire for me, for He called whom He wanted. But oh! the glory that I saw in that condition still so engaged my heart that I could seldom read of any that Christ called but I would wish, *If I had been in their clothes, if I had been born Peter or John, or if I had been nearby and heard Him when He called them, how would I have cried, "O Lord, call me also."* But oh! I feared He would not call me.

76. The Lord let me go this way for many months and showed me neither that I was already called or would be hereafter. But at last, after much time and many groans to God that I might be made a partaker of the heavenly calling, this Word came to me: "I will acquit them of the guilt of bloodshed, whom I had not acquitted; for the LORD dwells in Zion" (Joel 3:21). These words I thought were sent to encourage me to still wait upon God and signified to me that the time might come when I would be converted to Christ.

77. About this time I began to tell those poor people in Bedford my condition. When they heard, they told Mr. Gifford about me, and he talked with me. He invited me to his house, where I could hear him confer with others about the dealings of God with the soul. From all this I still received more conviction, and from that time I began to see something of the inward wretchedness of my wicked heart as I never had before. Now I found that lusts and corruptions would strongly put themselves forward within me in the form of wicked thoughts and desires that I had not experienced before. My desire for heaven and life began to fail. I found also that whereas before my soul was full of longing after God, now my heart began to hanker after every foolish vanity. Indeed, my heart began to be careless, both of my soul and heaven; it would now continually hang back in every duty.

78. I thought I was growing worse and worse; now was I further from conversion than I had ever been before. I began to entertain discouragement in my heart that laid me low as hell. I could not believe that Christ had love for me; I could neither hear Him nor see Him nor feel Him nor savor any of His things. I was driven as by a tempest.

79. Sometimes I would tell my condition to the people of God, and when they heard about it, they would pity me and tell me of the promises. But they might as well have told me that I must reach the sun with my finger as have bidden me receive or rely upon the promise. All my sense and feeling were against me, and I saw I had a heart that would sin and that lay under a law that would condemn. . . .

81. In those days I found my heart shutting itself against the Lord and against His holy Word. I found my unbelief setting, as it were, the shoulder to the door to keep Him out, even when I cried with many a bitter sigh, "Good Lord, break it open; Lord, break these gates of brass, and cut these bars of iron in two" (see Psalm 107:16), yet this word would sometimes create in my heart a peaceable pause: "I will gird you, though you have not known Me" (Isaiah 45:5).

82. But all this while, regarding the act of sinning, I was never more tender than now. My conscience was sore and would smart at every touch. Oh, how gingerly did I then go in all I did or said! I found myself as on a miry bog that shook if I just stirred and was left there without God and Christ and the Spirit and all good things.

83. But though I had been such a great sinner before conversion, yet God never charged the guilt of the sins of my ignorance upon me; only He showed me I was lost if I did not have Christ, because I had been a sinner. I saw that I wanted a perfect righteousness to present me without fault before God, and this righteousness was nowhere to be found except in the person of Jesus Christ.

84. I was more loathsome in my own eyes than a toad, and I thought I was in God's eyes, too. Sin and corruption would as naturally bubble out of my heart as water would bubble out of a fountain. I thought now that everyone had a better heart than I had; I could have changed hearts with anybody. I thought none but the devil himself could equalize me for inward wickedness and pollution of mind. I fell at the sight of my own vileness into deep despair, for I concluded that this condition that I was in could not stand with a state of grace. *Sure*, I thought, *I am forsaken of God; sure I am given up to the devil and to a reprobate mind*. And thus I continued a long while, even for several years.

85. While I was thus afflicted with the fears of my own damnation, there were two things that made me wonder: the one was when I saw old people hunting after the things of this life, as if they were going to live here always; the other was when I found believers distressed and cast down when they experienced outward losses, like a husband, wife, or child. *Lord*, thought I, *what fuss is here about such little things as these! What seeking after carnal things by some, and what*

*grief in others for the loss of them! If they labor
so much after the things of this present life and
spend so many tears for them, how am I to be
bemoaned, pitied, and prayed for! My soul is
dying. If my soul were in good condition, oh!
how rich I would esteem myself, though blessed
but with bread and water. I would count those
but small afflictions and would bear them as
little burdens. A wounded spirit who can bear?*

86. And though I was thus troubled with
the sense of my own wickedness, yet I was
afraid to let this sense go quite off my mind,
for I found that unless guilt of conscience
was removed in the right way, that is, by
the blood of Christ, a man grew worse for
the loss of his trouble of mind rather than
better. So if my guilt weighed me down,
then I would cry that the blood of Christ
might remove it; and if the guilt was lifting
without the blood of Christ, then I would
also strive to fetch it back upon my heart by
bringing the punishment for sin in hellfire
upon my spirit. I would cry, "Lord, let it
not go from my heart but by the blood of
Christ and by the application of Your mercy,

through Him, to my soul," for this scripture lay much upon me: "Without shedding of blood there is no remission" (Hebrews 9:22). I had seen some who, when they were under wounds of conscience, would cry and pray; but seeking immediate ease from their trouble rather than pardon for their sin, they cared not how they lost their guilt as long as they got it out of their mind. Therefore, having gotten rid of it the wrong way, it was not sanctified to them, but they grew harder and blinder and more wicked. This made me afraid and made me cry to God the more that it might not be so with me.

87. And now was I sorry that God had made me a man, for I feared I was a reprobate. I counted unconverted man as the saddest of all the creatures.

88. I thought it impossible that I should ever attain to so much goodness of heart as to thank God that He had made me a man. Man indeed is the most noble of all creatures in the visible world, but by sin he has made himself the most ignoble. The beasts, birds, fishes, etc., I blessed their condition, for they do not have a sinful nature, they are not obnoxious in the sight of God. They do not go to hellfire after death; I could therefore have rejoiced if my condition had been like any of theirs.

89. In this condition I went a great while; but when comforting time was come, I heard one preach a sermon on Song of Solomon 4:1: "Behold, you are fair, my love! Behold, you are fair!" But at that time he made "My love" his chief subject matter. From those words, after he had expounded on the text a little, he observed these conclusions: (1) the Church, and so every saved soul, is Christ's love, when loveless; (2) Christ's love is without a cause; (3) Christ's love when hated of the world; (4) Christ's love when under temptation and under desertion; (5) Christ's love from first to last.

90. But I got nothing out of what he said at first, but when he came to the application of the fourth particular, this was the word he said: "If the saved soul is Christ's love when under temptation and desertion, then, poor tempted soul, when you are assaulted and afflicted with temptation and the hiding of God's face, think on these three words, 'My love, still.' "

91. So as I was going home, these words came again into my thoughts, and I said in my heart, *What shall I get by thinking on these two words?* This thought had no sooner passed through my heart than these words began to kindle in my spirit: "You are My love, you are My love," twenty times, and still as they ran through my mind, they grew stronger and warmer and began to make me look up. But being as yet between hope and fear, I still replied in my heart, "But is it true, but is it true?" At which, this sentence fell upon me: "[He] did not know that what was done by the angel was real" (Acts 12:9).

92. Then I began to give place to the word, which, with power, made this joyful sound over and over within my soul, "You are My love, you are My love; and nothing shall separate you from My love." And with that,

Romans 8:39 came into my mind. Now was my heart filled full of comfort and hope, and now I could believe that my sins would be forgiven me. Indeed, I was now so taken with the love and mercy of God that I remember I could not contain myself till I got home. I thought I could have spoken of His love and His mercy to me even to the crows that sat upon the ploughed lands before me, had they been capable of understanding me. I said in my soul with much gladness, *Well, I wish I had a pen and ink here, I would write this down before I go any farther, for surely I will not forget this forty years from now.* But alas! within less than forty days, I began to question all again, which made me begin to question everything.

93. Yet still at times I was helped to believe that it was a true manifestation of grace to my soul, though I had lost much of the life and savor of it. Now about a week or two after this, I kept thinking of this scripture: "Simon, Simon! Indeed Satan has asked for you" (Luke 22:31). And sometimes it would sound so loud within me that once I looked over my shoulder, thinking that some man behind me had called to me. It came, as I have thought since, to stir me up to prayer and to watchfulness; it came to let me know that a storm was coming down upon me, but I understood it not.

94. That time that it called to me so loud was the last time that it sounded in my ear; but I think I still hear how loud a voice these words—"Simon, Simon"—sounded in my ears. I thought that somebody half a mile behind me had called after me, and although that was not my name, yet it made me suddenly look behind me, believing that he who called so loud meant me.

95. But so foolish and ignorant was I that I knew not the reason for this sound. As I saw and felt soon after, it was sent from heaven as an alarm to awaken me to prepare for what was coming, only it made me wonder what would be the reason that this scripture should still be sounding in my ears so often and so loud.

96. About a month later, a great storm came down upon me which was twenty times worse than all I had met with before. It came stealing upon me. First, all my comfort was taken from me, and then darkness seized upon me, after which whole floods of blasphemies against God, Christ, and the scriptures were poured upon my spirit, to my great confusion and astonishment. These blasphemous thoughts also stirred up questions in me against the very being of God and His only beloved Son, as in whether there were a God or Christ, and whether the holy scriptures were a fable and cunning story rather than the holy and pure Word of God.

97. The tempter would also assault me much with this thought: "How can you tell that the Turks don't have as good scriptures to prove their Mahomet is the Savior as we have to prove our Jesus is?" And how could I think that so many tens of thousands in so many countries and kingdoms should be without the knowledge of the right way to heaven, if there were indeed a heaven, and that we only, who live in a corner of the earth, should be blessed therewith? Everyone thinks his own religion the most right.

98. Sometimes I have endeavored to argue against these suggestions and to set some of the sentences of blessed Paul against them; but when I did this, these arguments would quickly return on me: Though we have made such a big deal of Paul and his words, how could I tell if he, being a cunning man, might not have chosen to deceive with strong delusions and also take pains to undo and destroy his fellow man? . . .

100. Only the distaste my spirit had for these thoughts made me refuse to embrace them. But this consideration I had only when God gave me a moment to swallow my spit, otherwise the noise and force of these temptations would drown out and bury all such thoughts or the remembrance of any such thing. While I was suffering this temptation, I often found my mind suddenly provoked to curse and swear or to speak some grievous thing against God or Christ and the scriptures.

101. *Now,* I thought, *surely I am possessed of the devil.* At other times I thought I must have lost my wits, for instead of lauding and magnifying the Lord with others when I heard Him spoken of, presently some most horrible blasphemous thought would bolt out of my heart against Him.

102. These things sank me into very deep despair, for I concluded that such things could not possibly be found among those who love God. I often compared myself to a child whom some gypsy has taken under her apron by force and is carrying away from friend and country. Kick sometimes I did, and also scream and cry, yet I was still bound in the wings of the temptation and the wind would carry me away. I thought also of Saul and of the evil spirit that possessed him and greatly feared that my condition was the same as his (1 Samuel 16:14).

103. In those days, when I heard others talk about what the sin against the Holy Spirit was, then the tempter would so provoke me to desire to sin that sin that it was as if I could not be quiet until I had committed it. So strong was this temptation upon me that often I was ready to clap my hand under my chin to keep my mouth from opening.

104. Now I blessed the condition of the dog and toad, and considered the state of everything that God had made far better than this dreadful state of mine was. Indeed, gladly would I have been in the condition of dog or horse, for they had no soul to perish under the everlasting weights of hell for sin, as mine was likely to. And though I saw this, felt this, and was broken to pieces with it, yet what added to my sorrow was that I could not find that I desired deliverance with all my soul. This scripture also tore up my soul: " 'There is no peace,' says the LORD, 'for the wicked' " (Isaiah 48:22). . . .

106. While this temptation lasted, which was about a year, I could attend to none of the ordinances of God without sore and great affliction. Indeed, then was I most distressed with blasphemies. If I had been hearing the Word, then uncleanness, blasphemies, and despair would hold me captive. If I had been reading, then sometimes I had sudden thoughts to question all I read. Sometimes my mind would be so strangely snatched away and possessed with other things that I have neither known, nor regarded, nor remembered.

107. In prayer, also, I was greatly troubled at this time. Sometimes I thought I saw the devil, thought I felt him behind me pulling on my clothes. He would also be at me continually in the time of prayer to be and stay no longer, drawing my mind away. Sometimes he would cast in such wicked thoughts as this: that I must pray to him or for him.

108. Also, when I would labor to fix my mind on God, the tempter would distract me and turn away my mind by presenting to my heart the image of a bush, a bull, a broom, or the like, as if I should pray to those. To these he would also at times so hold my mind that it was as if I could think of nothing else or pray to nothing else but to these.

109. Yet at times I would have some strong and heart-affecting apprehensions of God and the reality of the truth of His Gospel; but, oh! how would my heart, at such times, put forth itself with inexpressible groanings. My whole soul was then in every word; I would cry with pangs after God that He would be merciful to me. But then I would be daunted again with such thoughts as these: I would think that God mocked at my prayers, saying in the audience of the angels, "This poor, simple wretch hankers after Me as if I had nothing to do with My mercy but to bestow it on such as he. Poor fool! how deceived you are. It is not for such as you to have favor with the Highest."

110. Then the tempter came upon me with such discouragements as these: "You are very hot for mercy, but I will cool you. This frame of mind will not last forever. Many have been as hot as you, but I have quenched their zeal." And with this, people who had fallen away from the faith would be set before my eyes. Then I would be afraid that I would do so, too. *But*, thought I, *I*

*am glad this comes into my mind. I will watch
and take what precautions I can.* "Though
you do," said Satan, "I will be too hard for
you; I will cool you insensibly, by degrees,
little by little. What care I, though I be
seven years in chilling your heart, if I can do
it at last? I will have my end accomplished.
Though you be burning hot at present, yet if
I can pull you from this fire, I will have you
cold before long."

111. These thoughts distressed me greatly,
for as I could not yet find myself ready
for death, I thought to live long would
make me yet more unfit, for time would
make me forget all and wear away even the
remembrance of the evil of sin, the worth
of heaven, and the need I had for the blood
of Christ to wash me. But I thank Christ
Jesus that these things did not make me
stop crying but rather made me cry more.
In those days this was a good word to me:
"For I am persuaded that neither death nor
life, nor angels nor principalities nor powers,
nor things present nor things to come, nor
height nor depth, nor any other created

thing, shall be able to separate us from the love of God which is in Christ Jesus our Lord" (Romans 8:38–39). And now I hoped long life would not destroy me nor make me miss heaven.

112. Yet I had some supports in this temptation. The first verse of the third chapter of Jeremiah was something to me, and so was the consideration of the fifth verse of that chapter, that though we have spoken and done as evil things as we could, yet we should cry to God, "My Father, You are the guide of my youth," and should return to Him.

113. I had also a sweet glance from 2 Corinthians 5:21: "For He made Him who knew no sin to be sin for us, that we might become the righteousness of God in Him." One day as I was sitting in a neighbor's house, feeling very sad at the consideration of my many blasphemies and saying in my mind, *What ground have I to think that I, who have been so vile, should ever inherit eternal life?* this word came suddenly upon me: "What then shall we say to these things? If God is for us, who can be against us?" (Romans 8:31). This verse also was a help to me: "Because I live, you will live also" (John 14:19). But these were but hints, touches, and short visits, though very sweet when present, only they lasted not.

114. But afterwards the Lord more fully and graciously revealed Himself to me and not only delivered me from the guilt that was laid on my conscience by these things but also from the very filth thereof. The temptation was removed, and I was put into my right mind again.

115. One day, as I was traveling into the country and musing on the wickedness of my heart and considering the enmity that was in me toward God, this scripture came to my mind: "[He has] made peace through the blood of His cross" (Colossians 1:20). By this I was made to see, again and again, that God and my soul were friends by this blood; indeed, I saw that the justice of God and my sinful soul could embrace and kiss each other through this blood. That was a good day to me; I hope I shall never forget it.

116. Another time, as I sat by the fire in my house and mused on my wretchedness, the Lord made this also a precious word to me: "Inasmuch then as the children have partaken of flesh and blood, He Himself likewise shared in the same, that through death He might destroy him who had the power of death, that is, the devil, and release those who through fear of death were all their lifetime subject to bondage" (Hebrews 2:14–15). I thought that the glory of these words was so weighty on me that I was ready to swoon where I sat, yet not with grief and trouble but with joy and peace.

117. At this time also I sat under the ministry of Mr. Gifford, whose doctrine, by God's grace, contributed much toward my stability. This man made it his business to urge the people of God to take special heed that we not believe any truth presented to us by any man but cry out to God that He would convince us of the reality thereof, and establish us therein, by His own Spirit, in the holy Word. For, said he, if you do otherwise, when temptations come, if you have not strongly received the truth with evidence from heaven, you will find you lack the help and strength to resist that you once thought you had.

118. I had found, by sad experience, the truth of his words. I found my soul, through grace, very able to drink in this doctrine and inclined to pray to God that He would allow me to be without confirmation from heaven in nothing that pertained to God's glory and my own eternal happiness.

119. But oh! how was my soul now led from truth to truth by God, even from the birth and cradle of the Son of God to His ascension and second coming from heaven to judge the world.

120. Truly, I then found that God was very good to me, for there was nothing that I cried to God to reveal to me but He was pleased to do it for me. I thought I saw with great evidence, from the writings of the four evangelists, the wonderful work of God in giving Jesus Christ to save us. It was as if I had seen Him born, as if I had seen Him grow up, as if I had seen Him walk through this world, from the cradle to His cross, to which also, when He came, I saw how gently He gave Himself to be hanged and nailed on it for my sins. . . .

126. It would take too long to tell you in particular how God established me in all the things of Christ and how He led me into His words, also how He opened them to me, made them shine before me, and comforted me over and over.

127. In general He was pleased to take this course with me: first, to allow me to be afflicted with temptation concerning them and then reveal them to me. Sometimes I would lie under great guilt for sin, and then the Lord would show me the death of Christ and so sprinkle my conscience with His blood that I would find, before I was aware, that in that conscience where just a moment ago the law reigned and raged, even there would abide the peace and love of God through Christ.

128. Now had I evidence, I thought, of my salvation from heaven; now I could remember this manifestation and the other discovery of grace with comfort, and I would often desire that the last day would come that I might forever be inflamed with the sight and joy and communion with Him whose head was crowned with thorns, whose face was spit on and body broken and soul made an offering for my sins. For whereas before, I lay continually trembling at the mouth of hell, now I thought I had gotten so far from it that I could scarcely see it when I looked back. *And oh*! thought I, *if only I were eighty years old now, that I might die quickly, that my soul might go to its rest.*

129. But before I had gotten thus far out of my temptations, I greatly longed to see the experience of an ancient godly man who had written some hundreds of years before I was born. Well, after many such longings in my mind, one day God put into my hand a book by Martin Luther. It was his comment on the Galatians. Now I was much pleased that such an old book had fallen into my hands. When I had perused it a little, I found my condition, in his experience, so largely and profoundly handled that it seemed as if his book had been written out of my heart. This made me marvel.

130. He also most gravely debated of the rise of these temptations, namely, blasphemy, desperation, and the like, showing that the law of Moses as well as the devil, death, and hell have a very great hand in them. This was, at first, very strange to me, but considering and watching, I found it so indeed.

131. And now I found that I loved Christ dearly; oh! I thought my soul cleaved to Him, my affections cleaved to Him, I felt love for Him as hot as fire. But I quickly found that my great love was but little and that I, who had, as I thought, such burning love for Jesus Christ, could let Him go again for a trifle. God can tell how to abase us and can hide pride from man. Quickly after this my love was tried.

132. For after the Lord had thus graciously delivered me from this great temptation and had set me down so sweetly in the faith of His holy Gospel and had given me such strong consolation and blessed evidence from heaven regarding my interest in His love through Christ, the tempter came upon me again, and this time with a more grievous temptation than before.

133. And that was to sell and part with this most blessed Christ, to exchange Him for the things of this life, for anything. The temptation lay upon me for the span of a year and followed me so continually that I was not rid of it for even one day, no, not sometimes for one hour in many days together, except when I was asleep.

134. And though, in my judgment, I was persuaded that those who were once in Christ could never lose Him forever—"The land shall not be sold permanently, for the land is Mine," says God (Leviticus 25:23)—yet it was a continual vexation to me to think that I could have so much as one such thought within me against a Christ who had done for me as He had done.

135. But it was neither my dislike of the thought nor yet any desire and endeavor to resist it that in the least abated the continuation or strength of it; for it always, in almost whatever I thought, intermixed itself in such a way that I could neither eat my food, stoop for a pin, chop a stick, or look at this or that, but still the temptation would come—*Sell Christ for this or sell Christ for that; sell Him, sell Him. . . .*

137. I was so afraid that I would give in to this temptation that by the very force of my mind in laboring to resist this wickedness, my very body also would be put into action by way of pushing or thrusting with my hands or elbows, still answering as fast as the destroyer said, "Sell Him"—"I will not, I will not, I will not, I will not; no, not for thousands, thousands, thousands of worlds." . . .

139. But to be brief, one morning, as I lay in my bed, I was most fiercely assaulted with this temptation, the wicked suggestion still running in my mind, *Sell Him, sell Him, sell Him, sell Him, sell Him*, as fast as a man could speak. Against it, in my mind, as at other times, I answered, *No, no, not for thousands, thousands, thousands*, at least twenty times together. But at last, after much striving, even until I was almost out of breath, I felt this thought pass through my heart, *Let Him go, if He will!* and I thought also that I felt my heart freely consent to it. Oh, the diligence of Satan! Oh, the desperateness of man's heart!

140. Now was the battle won, and down I fell into great guilt and fearful despair. Thus getting out of my bed, I went moping in the field with as heavy a heart as mortal man, I think, could bear. There, for two hours, I was like a man bereft of life and bound to eternal punishment.

141. This scripture seized upon my soul: "Or profane person like Esau, who for one morsel of food sold his birthright. For you know that afterward, when he wanted to inherit the blessing, he was rejected, for he found no place for repentance, though he sought it diligently with tears" (Hebrews 12:16–17).

142. Now was I as one bound; I felt myself shut up to the coming judgment. Nothing now for two years would abide with me but damnation and an expectation of damnation; I say, nothing now would abide with me but this, a few moments of relief, as in the sequel you will see.

143. These words were to my soul like fetters of brass to my legs, in the continual sound of which I went for several months together. But about ten or eleven o'clock one day, as I was walking under a hedge, full of sorrow and guilt, suddenly this sentence bolted in upon me: "The blood of Christ remits all guilt." At this I made a stand in my spirit, and with that, this word took hold of me: "The blood of Jesus Christ His Son cleanses us from all sin" (1 John 1:7).

144. Now I began to feel peace in my soul, and I thought I saw the tempter leer and sneak away from me, as if ashamed of what he had done. At the same time also my sin and the blood of Christ were represented this way to me: that my sin, when compared to the blood of Christ, was no more next to it than a little clod of dirt or stone was to the vast field I saw before me. This gave me good encouragement for the space of two or three hours. During this time also I thought I saw, by faith, the Son of God suffering for my sins; but because the vision tarried not, I sank in my spirit, under heavy guilt again.

145. But mostly I was under heavy guilt because of the aforementioned scripture, concerning Esau's selling of his birthright, for that scripture would fill my mind all day long, all week long, indeed, all the year long and hold me down, so that I could by no means lift myself up. When I would strive to turn to this scripture or that for relief, still that sentence would be sounding in me, "For you know that afterward, when he wanted to inherit the blessing, he was rejected, for he found no place for repentance, though he sought it diligently with tears."

146. Sometimes I would have a touch from Luke 22:32, " 'I have prayed for you, that your faith should not fail' "; but it would not stay with me, neither could I, when I considered my state, find ground to believe in the least that there should be the root of that grace within me, having sinned as I had done. Now was I torn for many days.

147. Then began I with sad and careful heart to consider the nature of my sin and to search the Word of God for a word of promise or any encouraging sentence by which I might find relief. I began to consider this verse in Mark: " 'All sins will be forgiven the sons of men, and whatever blasphemies they may utter' " (Mark 3:28). At first I thought it contained a glorious promise for the pardon of high offences; but considering the place more fully, I thought it was rather to be understood as relating more chiefly to those who had, while in a natural state, committed such things as are mentioned there, but not to me, who had not only received light and mercy but had so slighted Christ as I had done.

148. I feared, therefore, that this wicked sin of mine might be that unpardonable sin of which he speaks there: " 'But he who blasphemes against the Holy Spirit never has forgiveness, but is subject to eternal condemnation' " (Mark 3:29). And I gave credit to this because of that sentence in Hebrews, "For you know that afterward, when he wanted to inherit the blessing, he was rejected, for he found no place for repentance, though he sought it diligently with tears" (Hebrews 12:17). And this stuck always with me.

149. And now was I both a burden and a terror to myself and was weary of my life yet afraid to die. Oh, how gladly would I have been anybody but myself! Anything but a man! And in any condition but my own! For nothing passed more frequently through my mind than that it was impossible for me to be forgiven my transgression and to be saved from the wrath to come. . . .

151. Then, being unwilling to perish, I began to compare my sin with others to see if any of those who were saved had done as I had done. So I considered David's adultery and murder and found them most heinous crimes, and those committed after light and grace had been received. But as I considered this, I perceived that his transgressions were only against the law of Moses, from which the Lord Christ could, with the consent of His Word, deliver him, but mine was against the Gospel; I had sold my Savior.

152. Now again was I tortured in my spirit when I considered that, besides the guilt that possessed me, I should be so devoid of grace, so bewitched. *What?* thought I, *must it be no sin but this? Must it be the great transgression* (Psalm 19:13)*? Must that wicked one touch my soul* (1 John 5:18)? Oh, what stings did I find in all these sentences!

153. *What?* thought I, *is there only one sin that is unpardonable? Only one sin that lays the soul beyond the reach of God's mercy, and must I be guilty of that? Must it be that? Is there only one sin among so many millions of sins for which there is no forgiveness, and must I commit it?* Oh, unhappy sin! Oh, unhappy man! These things so broke and confounded my spirit that I could not tell what to do. I thought, at times, they would rob me of my wits; and still, to aggravate my misery, this would run in my mind: "You know that afterward, when he wanted to inherit the blessing, he was rejected." Oh! No one knows the terrors of those days but myself.

154. After this I came to consider Peter's sin that he committed in denying his Master; for he had denied his Savior, as had I, and that after receiving light and mercy and, indeed, after being warned. I also considered that he did it three times, and that after having time between each offense to consider. But though I put all these circumstances together so that, if possible, I might find help, yet I considered again that his was but a denial of his Master, but mine was a selling of my Savior. Therefore I thought that I came closer to Judas than to either David or Peter.

155. Here again my torment would afflict me; it would grind me, as it were, to powder to discern the preservation of God toward others while I fell into the snare. For in my consideration of other men's sins and comparing them with my own, I could see how God preserved them, despite their wickedness, and would not let them, as He had let me, become a son of hell.

156. But oh, how my soul, at this time, prized the preservation that God set about His people! Ah, how safely I saw them walk whom God had hedged in! They were within His care, protection, and special providence, though they were as bad as I by nature. Yet because He loved them, He would not allow them to fall beyond the range of mercy. But as for me, I was gone, I had done it; He would not preserve me nor keep me but allowed me, because I was a reprobate, to fall as I had. Now those blessed places that spoke of God's keeping His people shone like the sun before me, though not to comfort me but to show me the blessed state and heritage of those whom the Lord had blessed.

157. Now I saw that as God had His hand in all that happened to His elect, so He had His hand in all the temptations that they had to sin against Him, not to animate them to wickedness but to choose their temptations and troubles for them, and also to leave them, for a time, to only those sins that might not destroy but humble them, those that might put them in the way of the renewing of His mercy. But oh, what love, what care, what kindness and mercy I now saw, mixing itself with the most severe and dreadful of all God's ways toward His people! He let David, Hezekiah, Solomon, Peter, and others fall, but He did not let them fall into sin unpardonable nor into hell for sin. *Oh!* thought I, *these are the men whom God has loved; these are the men whom God keeps in safety by Him, though He* *chastises them, and those whom He causes to abide under the shadow of the Almighty.* But all these thoughts added sorrow, grief, and horror to me, as whatever I now thought about was death to me. If I thought how God kept His own, that was death to me. If I thought of how I was falling myself, that was death to me. As all things worked together for the best and for the good of those who were called according to His purpose, so I thought that all things worked for my damage and for my eternal overthrow.

158. Again I began to compare my sin with the sin of Judas, that, if possible, I might find that mine differed from that which, in truth, is unpardonable. By considering, I found that Judas did his intentionally, but mine was against my prayer and strivings. Besides, his was committed with much deliberation but mine all of a sudden. All this time I was tossed to and fro, like the locusts, and driven from trouble to sorrow.

159. Yet this consideration about Judas and his sin was, for a while, some small relief to me, for I saw I had not transgressed as badly as he. But this relief was quickly gone again, for I thought there might be more ways than one to commit the unpardonable sin. Also I thought that there might be degrees of that transgression, as well as of others; wherefore, for all I could yet perceive, this iniquity of mine might be such as might never be passed by.

160. I was often now ashamed of the thought that I might be like such an ugly man as Judas. I thought also how loathsome I would be to all the saints at the day of judgment. Now I could scarcely see a good man whom I believed had a good conscience but my heart would tremble while I was in his presence. Oh! now I saw a glory in walking with God and what a mercy it was to have a good conscience before Him.

161. I was much tempted about this time to content myself with the false opinion that there was no such thing as a day of judgment, that we will not rise again, and that sin was not such a grievous thing. The tempter suggested this: "For if these things are indeed true, yet to believe otherwise would yield you ease for the present. If you must perish, do not torment yourself so much beforehand; drive the thoughts of damning out of your mind by filling your mind with some such conclusions that atheists use."

162. But oh! when such thoughts went through my heart and death and judgment were in my view, I thought the judge stood at the door, so such thoughts could not be entertained. But I thought I saw by this that Satan will use any means to keep the soul from Christ; he does not love an awakened frame of spirit. Security, blindness, darkness, and error are the very kingdom of the wicked one.

163. I found it hard work now to pray because despair was swallowing me up; I thought I was driven away from God, for always when I cried to God for mercy, this thought would come in: *It is too late; I am lost; God has let me fall, not for my correction but for my condemnation. My sin is unpardonable, and I know, concerning Esau, how after he had sold his birthright, he wanted to receive the blessing but was rejected.*

164. Then was I struck by a very great trembling, insomuch that sometimes I could feel my body and mind, for whole days together, shake and totter under the sense of the dreadful judgment of God that will fall on those who have sinned that most fearful and unpardonable sin. I felt also such a heat in my stomach because of my terror that it was as if my breast bone had been split in two. . . .

166. Yet this saying would sometimes come to my mind: "You have received gifts among men, even from the rebellious" (Psalm 68:18). *The rebellious,* thought I, *why, surely they are those who were once under subjection to their prince, even those who, after they have sworn subjection to his government, have taken up arms against him. And this,* thought I, *is* *my very condition; once I loved Him, feared Him, served Him, but now I am a rebel. I have sold Him, I have said, "Let Him go if He will;" but yet He has gifts for rebels, and then why not for me? . . . .*

168. Again, after I had considered the sins of the saints and found mine were worse than theirs, I began to think within myself: *If I put all theirs together and mine against theirs, might I not then find some encouragement? For if mine, though bigger than anyone's, is still just equal to all, then there is hope, for that blood that has virtue enough in it to wash away all theirs also has virtue enough in it to do away with mine.* Here again I would consider the sin of David, of Solomon, of Manasseh, of Peter, and the rest of the great offenders, and would also labor to heighten their sins by several circumstances, but, alas! it was all in vain. . . .

172. This one consideration would always kill my heart: My sin was point-blank against my Savior; I had in my heart said of Him, "Let Him go if He will." Oh! I thought this sin was bigger than the sins of a country, of a kingdom, or of the whole world.

173. Now I would find my mind fleeing from God, as from the face of a dreadful judge; yet this was my torment: I could not escape His hand. "It is a fearful thing to fall into the hands of the living God" (Hebrews 10:31). But blessed be His grace, this scripture would call, as if running after me, "'I have blotted out, like a thick cloud, your transgressions, and like a cloud, your sins. Return to Me, for I have redeemed you'" (Isaiah 44:22). This scripture would come to my mind when I was fleeing from the face of God; for I did flee from His face, that is, my mind and spirit fled from Him because I could not endure His highness. Then would the text cry, "Return to Me, for I have redeemed you." Indeed, this would make me stop for a moment and, as it were, look over my shoulder behind me, to see if I could discern that the God of grace followed me with a pardon in His hand, but I could no sooner do that than all would be clouded and darkened again by that sentence, "For you know that afterward, when he wanted to inherit the blessing, he found no place of repentance, though he sought it carefully with tears." So I could not return but fled, though sometimes it cried "Return, return!" But I feared to turn to it, in case it did not come from God.

174. Once as I was walking to and fro in a man's shop, afflicting myself with self-abhorrence for this wicked thought, greatly fearing I would not be pardoned, and praying that if this sin of mine differed from the sin against the Holy Ghost, the Lord would show it to me. And being now ready to sink with fear, suddenly there was, as if there had rushed in at the window, the noise of wind upon me, but very pleasant, and I heard a voice speaking, "Did you ever refuse to be justified by the blood of Christ?" And right then my whole life and past were, in a moment, revealed to me, in which I was made to see that I had not. So my heart answered groaningly, *No*. Then fell, with power, this word of God upon me: "See that you do not refuse Him who speaks" (Hebrews 12:25). This scripture seized my spirit strangely; it brought light with it and commanded silence in my heart of all those tumultuous thoughts that used to roar and bellow like masterless hell-hounds and make a hideous noise within me. It showed me, also, that Jesus Christ had yet a word of grace and mercy for me, that He had not, as I had feared, quite forsaken my soul. Indeed, this was a kind of reprimand for my proneness to desperation, a kind of threatening of me if I did not venture my salvation on the Son of God, notwithstanding my heinous sins. But as to my figuring out this strange dispensation, what it was I knew not. I have not yet, in twenty years' time, been able to make a judgment of it. I thought then what here I am reluctant to speak. Truly that sudden rushing wind was as if an angel had come upon me, but both it and the salvation I will leave until the day of judgment. Only this I say, it commanded a great calm in my soul, it persuaded me there might be hope. It showed me what the unpardonable sin was, and that my soul had yet the blessed privilege to flee to Jesus for mercy. But concerning this dispensation, I know not yet what to say about it. I leave it to be thought about by men of sound judgment. I lay not the stress of my salvation on it but on the Lord Jesus; yet, seeing I am here unfolding my secret things, I thought it might not be altogether inexpedient to let this also show itself. This feeling lasted for about three or four days, and then I began to despair again.

175. My life still hung in doubt before me, not knowing which way I would tip. I found my soul's desire was to cast itself at the foot of grace, by prayer and supplication. But oh! it was hard for me now to pray to this Christ for mercy, against whom I had most vilely sinned. It was hard work to look Him in the face. Indeed, I have found it as difficult to come to God by prayer, after backsliding from Him, as to do any other thing. Oh, the shame that now attended me! But I saw there was but one way for me: I must go to Him and humble myself before Him and beg that He would show pity to me and have mercy on my wretched, sinful soul.

176. When the tempter perceived this, he strongly suggested to me that I ought not to pray to God, for prayer was not for people in my case, neither could it do me any good, because I had rejected the Mediator, by whom all prayer came with acceptance to God the Father, and without whom no prayer could come into His presence. Therefore now to pray was to add sin to sin, and seeing God had cast me off, it was the next way to anger and offend Him more than I ever had before.

177. "For God," said he, "has grown weary of you for these several years already, because you are not His. Your crying in His ears has not been a pleasant voice to Him, and, therefore, He let you sin this sin that you might be quite cut off, and will you pray still?" This the devil urged and reminded me that, in Numbers, when Moses said to the children of Israel that because they would not go up to possess the land when God would have them, therefore, forever after, God barred them from there, though they prayed with tears that they might go in (Numbers 14:36–37, etc.).

178. As it is said in another place (Exodus 21:14), the man that sins presumptuously shall be taken from God's altar, that he may die, even as Joab was by King Solomon when he thought to find shelter there (1 Kings 2:28, etc.). These scriptures pinched me sorely; yet, my case being desperate, I thought within myself, *I can but die, and if it must be so, it shall once be said that such a one died at the foot of Christ in prayer.* This I did, but with great difficulty, God knows, because that saying about Esau was still being set at my heart like a flaming sword to guard the way of the tree of life, lest I should taste thereof and live. Oh! who knows how hard a thing I found it to come to God in prayer.

179. I also desired the prayers of the people of God for me, but I feared that God would give them no heart to do it; indeed, I trembled in my soul to think that some of them would soon tell me that God had said those words to them that He once said to the prophet concerning the children of Israel, "Do not pray for this people," for I have rejected them (Jeremiah 11:14). So, do not pray for him, for I have rejected him. Indeed, I thought that He had whispered this to some of them already, only they dared not tell me so, neither dared I ask them about it, for fear that if it should be so, it would make me quite beside myself.

180. About this time I took an opportunity to share my mind with an ancient Christian and told him my case. I told him also that I was afraid that I had sinned the sin against the Holy Ghost, and he told me he thought so, too. Here, therefore, I had but cold comfort, but talking a little more with him, I found him, though a good man, a stranger to much combat with the devil. So I went to God again, as well as I could, for mercy still.

181. Now also the tempter began to mock me in my misery, saying that since I had parted with the Lord Jesus and provoked Him to displeasure, who would have stood between my soul and the flame of devouring fire, there was now but one way and that was to pray that God the Father would be the

Mediator between His Son and me, that we might be reconciled again and that I might have that blessed benefit in Him that His saints enjoyed.

182. Then this scripture seized upon my soul: "He is unique, and who can make Him change?" (Job 23:13). Oh! I saw it was as easy to persuade Him to make a new world, a new covenant, or a new Bible as to pray for such a thing. This was to persuade Him that what He had done already was mere folly, and to persuade Him to alter, indeed, to disannul, the whole way of salvation. Then would this saying rip my soul in two, "Nor is there salvation in any other, for there is no other name under heaven given among men by which we must be saved" (Acts 4:12).

183. Now the most free, full, and gracious words of the Gospel were the greatest torment to me; indeed, nothing so afflicted me as thoughts of Jesus Christ, because I had cast Him off. Every time I thought of the Lord Jesus, of His grace, love, goodness, kindness, gentleness, meekness, death, blood, promises and blessed exhortations, comforts and consolations, they struck my soul like a sword, for still these thoughts would make a place for themselves in my heart: *Aye, this is the Jesus, the loving Savior, the Son of God, whom you have parted with, whom you slighted, despised, and abused. This is the only Savior, the only Redeemer, the only one who could so love sinners as to wash them from their sins in His own most precious blood; but you have no part nor lot in this Jesus; you have put Him away from you; you have said in your heart, "Let Him go if He will." Now, therefore, you are cut off from Him; you have cut yourself off from Him. Behold, then, His goodness, but you yourself cannot be a partaker of it. Oh,* thought I, *what have I lost! What have I parted with! What have I disinherited my poor soul of!* Oh! it is sad to be destroyed by the grace and mercy of God, to have the Lamb, the Savior, turn lion and destroyer (Revelation 6). I also trembled, as I have said, at the sight of the saints of God, especially at those who greatly loved Him and who made it their business to walk continually with Him in this world, for by their words, their actions, and all their expressions of tenderness and fear to sin against their precious Savior, they laid guilt on me and added affliction and shame to my soul.

184. Now the tempter began to mock my soul another way, saying that Christ did indeed pity my case and was sorry for my loss, but because I had sinned as I had, He could not help me or save me, for my sin was not of the nature of theirs for whom He bled and died or counted with those who were laid to His charge when He hung on the cross. Therefore, unless He could come down from heaven and die again for this sin, I could gain no benefit from Him, though He greatly pitied me. These things may seem ridiculous to others, but to me they were most tormenting cogitations. To think that Jesus Christ could have so much love as to pity me when He could not help me augmented my misery; nor did I think that the reason why He could not help me was because His merits were weak or His grace and salvation spent on them already, but because His faithfulness to His threatening would not let Him extend His mercy to me. Besides, as I have already hinted, I thought that my sin was not within the bounds of that pardon that was wrapped up in a promise; and if it was not, then I knew that it was easier for heaven and earth to pass away than for me to have eternal life. So the ground of all these fears of mine arose from a steadfast belief that I had of the stability of the holy Word of God and also from my being misinformed of the nature of my sin.

185. These thoughts would so confound me and imprison me that I knew not what to do; but, oh! I thought, that He would come down again! Oh! that the work of man's redemption was yet to be done by Christ! How would I pray Him and entreat Him to count this sin among the rest for whom He died! But this scripture would strike me down as dead, "Christ, having been raised from the dead, dies no more. Death no longer has dominion over Him" (Romans 6:9).

186. Thus by the assaults of the tempter was my soul, like a broken vessel, driven as with the winds and tossed sometimes headlong into despair, sometimes upon the covenant of works and sometimes to wish that the new covenant, and the conditions thereof, might be turned another way and changed. But in all these I was like those who are dashed against the rocks, more broken and scattered. Oh, the fears and terrors that come with a thorough application of guilt yielded to desperation! This is the man who had his dwelling among the tombs, always crying out and cutting himself with stones (Mark 5:2–5). But all in vain; desperation will not comfort him; the old covenant will not save him; no, heaven and earth will pass away before one jot or tittle of the Word and law of grace will fall or be removed. This I saw, this I felt, and under this I groaned; yet this advantage I gained: namely, a further confirmation of the certainty of the way of salvation and a firmer belief that the scriptures were the Word of God! Oh! I cannot now express what then I saw and felt of the steadiness of Jesus Christ, the Rock of man's salvation. What was done could not be undone, added to, or altered. I saw, indeed, that sin might drive the soul beyond Christ, even the sin that is unpardonable, but woe to him who was so driven, for the Word would shut him out.

187. One day I walked to a neighboring town, sat down on a bench in the street, and fell into deep thought about the most fearful state my sin had brought me to. After long musing, I lifted up my head, but I saw that it was as if the sun begrudged to give light and as if the very stones in the street and tiles upon the houses bent themselves against me. I thought that they all conspired together to banish me out of the world; I was abhorred by them and unfit to dwell among them or to be partaker of their benefits because I had sinned against the Savior. Oh, how happy now was every creature over what I was, for they stood fast and kept their station, but I was gone and lost.

188. Then breaking out in the bitterness of my soul, I said to myself, "How can God comfort such a wretch as I?" I had no sooner said it than this returned to me, as an echo answers a voice: "This sin is not unto death." At this I felt as if I had been raised out of a grave and cried out again, "Lord, how could You find out such a word as this?" For I was filled with admiration at the unexpectedness of the sentence, the fitness of the word, the rightness of the timing of it. The power and sweetness and light and glory that came with it were marvelous to me. I now had, for the time, no doubts about what I had been so much in doubt before. My fears before were that my sin was unpardonable, so I had no right to pray or to repent, or that if I did, it would be of no advantage to me. *But now*, thought I, *if this sin is not unto death, then it is pardonable; therefore, from this I have encouragement to come to God by Christ for mercy, to consider the promise of forgiveness as that which stands with open arms to receive me, as well as others*. This, therefore, brought great ease to my mind. Only those who know by their own experience what my trouble was can tell what relief came to my soul; it was a release to me from my former bonds and a shelter from my former storm. I seemed now to stand upon the same ground with other sinners and to have as much a right to the Word and prayer as any of them.

189. Now I was hopeful that my sin was not unpardonable and that there might be hope for me to obtain forgiveness. But oh, how Satan tried to bring me down again! But he could by no means do it, neither that day nor most of the next. Yet toward the evening of the next day, I felt this word begin to leave me and to withdraw its support from me, and so I returned to my old fears again, but with a great deal of grudging, for I feared the sorrow of despair, and my faith could no longer retain this word.

190. But the next day, at evening, I went to seek the Lord, and as I prayed, my soul cried to Him these words, with strong cries: "O Lord, show me that You have loved me with an everlasting love" (Jeremiah 31:3). I had no sooner said it than this response came to me with sweetness: "I have loved you with an everlasting love." Now I went to bed at peace; also, when I awoke the next morning, it was fresh upon my soul—and I believed it.

191. But still the tempter did not leave me, for it could not be less than a hundred times that he labored that day to break my peace. Oh! the combats and conflicts that I then met with as I strove to hold on to this word. Yet God bore me up and kept my heart upon it, from which I had also, for several days, much sweetness and hope of pardon. For thus it was made out to me, "I loved you while you were committing this sin, I loved you before, I love you still, and I will love you forever."

192. Yet I saw my sin as a filthy crime and could not help concluding with great shame and astonishment that I had horribly abused the holy Son of God. I felt my soul greatly love Him and my heart yearn for Him, for I saw He was still my Friend and rewarded me good for evil. Indeed, the love and affection that then burned within me toward my Lord and Savior Jesus Christ worked, at this time, such a strong and hot desire of revenge upon myself for the abuse I had done to Him that if I had had a thousand gallons of blood within my veins, I could have freely spilled it all at the command and feet of my Lord and Savior.

193. As I was considering in my musings and studies how to love the Lord and to express my love to Him, this saying came to me: "If You, LORD, should mark iniquities, O Lord, who could stand? But there is forgiveness with You, that You may be feared" (Psalm 130:3–4). These were good words to me, especially the latter part, that is, that there is forgiveness with the Lord, that He might be feared. As I then understood it, it was that He might be loved and held in reverence, for it was thus revealed to me that God sets so high an esteem upon the love of His poor creatures that rather than going without their love, He pardons their transgressions.

194. And now was this word fulfilled for me, and I was refreshed by it: " 'That you may remember and be ashamed, and never open your mouth anymore because of your shame, when I provide you an atonement for all you have done,' says the Lord GOD" (Ezekiel 16:63). Thus was my soul at this time and forever, as I then thought, set at liberty from being again afflicted with my former guilt.

195. But before many weeks were over I began to despond again, fearing that, notwithstanding all that I had enjoyed, I might yet be deceived and destroyed at the last. For this consideration came strong into my mind: that whatever comfort and peace I thought I might have from the word of the promise of life, unless there could be found in my refreshment a concurrence and agreement in the scriptures, let me think whatever I wanted and hold it fast, I would find no such thing at the end, for "the Scripture cannot be broken" (John 10:35).

196. Now began my heart to ache again and fear that I might meet with disappointment at the end, so I began, with all seriousness, to examine my former comfort and to consider whether one who had sinned as I had might with confidence trust in the faithfulness of God, laid down in those words by which I had been comforted and on which I had leaned. But now were brought to my mind these sayings: "For it is impossible for those who were once enlightened, and have tasted the heavenly gift, and have become partakers of the Holy Spirit, and have tasted the good word of God and the powers of the age to come, if they fall away, to renew them again to repentance" (Hebrews 6:4–6). For if we sin willfully after we have received the knowledge of the truth, "there no longer remains a sacrifice for sins, but a certain fearful expectation of judgment, and fiery indignation which will devour the adversaries" (Hebrews 10:26–27).

197. Now was the word of the Gospel forced from my soul, so that no promise or encouragement was to be found in the Bible for me; and now would that saying work upon my spirit to afflict me, "Do not rejoice, O Israel, with joy like other peoples" (Hosea 9:1). For I saw indeed there was cause for rejoicing for those who held to Jesus, but as for me, I had cut myself off by my transgressions and left myself neither foothold nor handhold among all the stays and props in the precious Word of Life.

198. And truly I now felt myself to sink into a gulf, as a house whose foundation is destroyed. As soon as this fresh assault had fastened on my soul, this scripture came into my heart: "[This] refers to many days yet to come" (Daniel 10:14). And indeed I found it was so, for I could not be delivered or brought to peace again until two and a half years had passed. So these words, though in themselves they tended to cause discouragement, yet to me, who feared this condition would be eternal, they were sometimes a help and refreshment to me.

199. For, thought I, many days are not forever, many days will have an end, therefore seeing I was to be afflicted not a few but many days, I was glad it was but for many days.

200. Now while these scriptures lay before me, and laid sin anew at my door, that saying in the eighteenth of Luke, along with others, encouraged me to prayer. Then the tempter attacked me again, suggesting that neither the mercy of God nor the blood of Christ concerned me, nor could they give me help for my sin; therefore it was in vain to pray. *Yet*, thought I, *I will pray.* "But," said the tempter, "your sin is unpardonable." "Well," said I, "I will pray." "It is no good," said he. "Yet," said I, "I will pray." So I went to prayer to God, and while I was praying, I uttered words to this effect: "Lord, Satan tells me that neither Your mercy nor Christ's blood is sufficient to save my soul. Lord, shall I honor You most by believing You will and can? Or him, by believing You neither will nor can? Lord, I would gladly honor You by believing You will and can."

201. And as I was thus before the Lord, this scripture fastened on my heart: " 'O [man], great is your faith!' " (Matthew 15:28). As if one had clapped me on the back, I was on my knees before God. Yet I was not able to believe that this was a prayer of faith till almost six months later, for I could not think that I had faith or that there should be a word for me to act in faith on. Therefore I was still stuck in the jaws of desperation and went mourning up and down, crying, "Is His mercy completely gone?"

202. There was nothing now that I longed for more than to be delivered from doubt, and as I was vehemently desiring to know if there was indeed hope for me, these words came rolling into my mind: "Will the Lord cast off forever? And will He be favorable no more? Has His mercy ceased forever? Has His promise failed forevermore? Has God forgotten to be gracious? Has He in anger shut up His tender mercies?" (Psalm 77:7–9). And all the while they ran through my mind, I thought I had this still as the answer: "It is a question whether He has or not; it may be He has not." Indeed, the question seemed to me to carry in it a sure affirmation that indeed He had not nor would so cast off but would be favorable, that His promise does not fail and that He had not forgotten to be gracious nor would in anger shut up His tender mercy. . . .

204. One morning, when I was again at prayer and trembling in fear that no word of God could help me, this portion of a sentence darted in upon me: " 'My grace is sufficient' " (2 Corinthians 12:9). At this I thought I felt hope.

205. By these words I was sustained for seven or eight weeks, yet not without great conflicts, for my peace would come and go, sometimes twenty times a day.

206. Therefore I still prayed to God that He would come in with this scripture more fully on my heart, that is, that He would help me to apply the whole sentence, for as yet I could not. And though it came no further, it answered my former question, that is, that there was hope, yet because "for you" was left out, I was not content but prayed to God for that also. One day, as I was in a meeting of God's people, full of sadness and terror, as I was thinking my soul was no better, these words suddenly broke in on me with great power: "My grace is sufficient for you, My grace is sufficient for you, My grace is sufficient for you." And oh! I thought that every word was a mighty word to me.

207. My understanding was so enlightened that I felt as though I had seen the Lord Jesus look down on me from heaven and direct these words to me. This sent me home mourning; it broke my heart and filled me full of joy and laid me low as the dust. Only this glory and refreshing comfort did not stay long with me, yet it continued with me for several weeks and encouraged me to hope. But as soon as the powerful effect of it was taken from my heart, the other about Esau returned on me as before, so my soul hung as in a pair of scales again, sometimes up and sometimes down, now in peace and now in terror.

208. I went on like this for many weeks. Sometimes my torment would be very sore, for all those scriptures from Hebrews would be set before me as the only sentences that would keep me out of heaven. Then I would begin to repent that that thought ever went through me, and I would think, *Why, how many scriptures are there against me? There are only three or four, and cannot God overlook them and save me in spite of them?* Other times I would think, *Oh! if it were not for these three or four scriptures, now how might I be comforted?*

209. Then I thought I saw Peter, Paul, John, and all the writers look on me with scorn and hold me in derision, and it was as if they said to me, "All our words are truth, one of as much force as another. It is not we who have cut you off, but you have cast away yourself; there is not one of our sentences that you must take hold upon but these and ones like them: 'It is impossible; there remains no more sacrifice for sin' (Hebrews 6). 'It would have been better for them not to have known the way of righteousness, than having known it, to turn from the holy commandment delivered to them' " (2 Peter 2:21). . . .

211. I was confounded, not knowing what to do nor how to be satisfied in this question: Could the scriptures agree about the salvation of my soul? I quaked at the apostles; I knew their words were true and that they must stand forever.

212. One day I was considering how I felt about the nature of the several scriptures that came to my mind. When I thought about the one about grace, then was I quiet; but when I thought about the one about Esau, I was tormented. *Lord*, thought I, *if both these scriptures would meet in my heart at once, I would like to see which of them would get the better of me.* So I had a longing that they might both come to my mind at the same time and desired of God that they might.

213. Well, about two or three days later, they did indeed hit me at the same time and worked and struggled strangely in me for a while. At last, the verse about Esau's birthright began to grow weak and withdraw and vanish, and the one about the sufficiency of grace prevailed with peace and joy. And as I was musing, this scripture came home to me: "Mercy triumphs over judgment" (James 2:13).

214. This was a wonder to me, yet truly I am able to think it was of God, for the word of the law and wrath must give place to the word of life and grace; because, though the word of condemnation is glorious, yet the word of life and salvation far exceeds it in glory (2 Corinthians 3:8–12; Mark 9:5–7).

215. This scripture also most sweetly visited my soul: " 'The one who comes to Me I will by no means cast out' " (John 6:37). But Satan greatly labored to pull this promise from me, telling me that Christ did not mean me but sinners of a lower rank who had not done as I had done. But I would answer him, "Satan, there is in this word no such exception, but 'the one who comes'—any one—'the one who comes to me I will

by no means cast out.' " Of all the tricks that
Satan tried to take this scripture from me,
he never put out this question: "But do you
come in the right way?" And I have thought
the reason was because he thought I knew
full well what coming the right way was;
for I saw that to come the right way was to
come as I was, a vile and ungodly sinner,
and to cast myself at the feet of mercy,
condemning myself for sin. If ever Satan and
I strove for any word of God in all my life, it
was for this good word of Christ. Oh, what
work did we make! He pulled and I pulled,
but God be praised, I got the better of him.
I got some sweetness from it.

216. But in spite of all these helps and
blessed words of grace, the verse about Esau's
selling of his birthright still distressed my
conscience at times; for though I had been
most sweetly comforted, yet when that verse
came to my mind, it made me fear again.
Now I went another way to work so I could
consider the words. When I had considered
them, I found that if they were fairly taken,
they would amount to this: that I had freely

left the Lord Jesus Christ to His choice as to whether He would be my Savior or not. Then this scripture gave me hope: " 'I will never leave you nor forsake you' " (Hebrews 13:5). "O Lord," said I, "but I have left You." Then the verse answered again, "But I will not leave you." For this I thank God.

217. Yet I was grievously afraid He would, and I found it exceedingly hard to trust Him, seeing I had so offended Him. I would have been glad if this thought had never struck me, for then I thought I could have leaned on His grace with more ease and freedom. I see my problem was the same as that of Joseph's brothers: the guilt of their own wickedness often filled them with fears that their brother would despise them (Genesis 50:15–17).

218. But above all the scriptures that I came across, one in the twentieth chapter of Joshua was the greatest comfort to me, one that speaks of the killer who was to flee for refuge. And if the avenger of blood pursued the killer, then, said Moses, the elders of the city of refuge should not deliver him into his hand, because he smote his neighbor unknowingly and did not hate him beforehand. Oh, blessed be God for this word; I was convinced that I was the killer and that the avenger of blood pursued me. Only now I needed to inquire whether I had the right to enter the city of refuge. So I found that he who lay in wait to shed blood must not; it was he who unknowingly did it, he who accidentally shed blood, not out of spite or grudge or malice, even he who did not hate his neighbor before. Therefore:

219. I thought truly I was a man who could enter, because I had smitten my neighbor unwittingly and hated him not beforehand. I did not hate Him beforehand; no, I prayed to Him and had a tender conscience about sinning against Him. Indeed, against this wicked temptation I had striven for a year. Therefore I thought I had the right to enter this city, and the elders, who are the apostles, would not deliver me up. This, therefore, was great comfort to me and gave me much ground for hope.

220. Yet I had one question that my soul much desired to be resolved about: Is it possible for any soul who has sinned the unpardonable sin to receive the least true spiritual comfort from God through Christ? After I had considered this at great length, I found the answer was no, they could not, for these reasons:

221. First, because those who have sinned that sin are debarred from a share in the blood of Christ, and being shut out of that, they must be devoid of hope and spiritual comfort; for to such "there no longer remains a sacrifice for sins" (Hebrews 10:26). Secondly, because they are denied a share in the promise of life " 'it will not be forgiven him, either in this age or in the age to come' " (Matthew 12:32). Thirdly, the Son of God excludes them from a share in His blessed intercession, being forever ashamed to own them before His holy Father and the blessed angels in heaven (Mark 8:38).

222. When I had, with much deliberation, considered this matter and concluded that the Lord had comforted me, even after my wicked sin, then I dared venture to come near those most terrible scriptures that I had been so frightened of and on which I scarcely looked. But now I began to come close to them, to read them and consider them.

223. When I began to do this, they did not look as grim to me as I had thought. First, I came to the sixth chapter of the Hebrews, trembling with fear that it would strike me. When I had considered, I found that the falling there intended was a falling away completely, that is, an absolute denial of the Gospel of remission of sins by Christ. Secondly, I found that this falling away must be done openly, so as to put Christ to an open shame before the world. Thirdly, I found that the ones He there intended were forever cut off from God, in blindness, hardness, and impenitency; it is impossible for them to be renewed again to repentance. By all these particulars, I found, to God's everlasting praise, my sin was not the sin this passage spoke of.

> First, I confessed I was fallen but not fallen away, that is, from the profession of faith in Jesus to eternal life. Secondly, I confessed that I had put Jesus Christ to shame by my sin but not to open shame; I did not deny Him before men nor condemn Him as a fruitless one before the world. Thirdly, I did not find that God had cut me off or denied me to come, though I found it hard work indeed to come to Him by sorrow and repentance. Blessed be God for unsearchable grace.

224. Then I considered that verse in the tenth chapter of Hebrews and found that the willful sin there mentioned is not every willful sin but that which throws off Christ and His commandments. Secondly, it must also be done openly, before two or three witnesses, to answer to the law (verse 28). Thirdly, this sin cannot be committed without great spite against the Spirit of grace, despising both the dissuasions from that sin and the persuasions to the contrary. But though this sin of mine was devilish, the Lord knows it did not amount to these.

225. And regarding the verse in the twelfth chapter of Hebrews about Esau's selling his birthright, though this was the verse that stood like a spear against me, now I considered, first, that his was not a hasty thought but a thought consented to and put into practice, and that after some deliberation (Genesis 25). Secondly, it was a public and open action, even before his brother, if not before many more; this made his sin of a far more heinous nature than it would have been otherwise. Thirdly, he continued to slight his birthright: "Then he ate and drank, arose, and went his way. Thus Esau despised his birthright" (Genesis 25:34).

226. Now regarding the part about Esau seeking a place of repentance, I thought, first, this was not for the birthright but for the blessing; this is clear from the apostle and is distinguished by Esau himself: " 'He took away my birthright, and now look, he has taken away my blessing!' " (Genesis 27:36). Secondly, I came again to the apostle to see what might be the mind of God concerning Esau's sin. As far as I could figure, this was the mind of God: the birthright signified regeneration and the blessing signified the eternal inheritance, for so the apostle seems to hint: "lest there be any. . .profane person like Esau, who for one morsel of food sold his birthright" (Hebrews 12:16). It was as if he was saying, "Lest there be any person among you who will cast off all those blessed beginnings of God that are on him at present, leading to a new birth, lest they become like Esau, even be rejected afterwards when they want to inherit the blessing." . . .

228. When I had considered these scriptures and found that to understand them thus was not against but according to other scriptures, it added further to my encouragement and comfort and also gave a great blow to the objection that the scriptures could not agree about the salvation of my soul. And now remained only the end of the tempest, for the thunder had gone beyond me, only some drops still remained; but because my former anguish was very sore and deep, I thought every voice was "Fire, fire," just as it is for those who have been scared with fire, and every little touch hurt my tender conscience.

229. But one day, as I was passing a field, fearing that all was not right with my conscience, suddenly this sentence fell upon my soul, "Your righteousness is in heaven," and I thought I saw, with the eyes of my soul, Jesus Christ at God's right hand. There, I say, is my righteousness, so that wherever I was, or whatever I was doing, God could not say of me, "He wants my righteousness," for that was just before Him. I also saw, moreover, that it was not my good frame of heart that made my righteousness better nor yet my bad frame that made my righteousness worse, for my righteousness was Jesus Christ Himself, the same yesterday, and today, and forever (Hebrews 13:8).

230. Now did my chains fall off my legs indeed. I was set free from my affliction and irons, my temptations fled away. From that time, those dreadful scriptures of God stopped troubling me. I went home rejoicing over the grace and love of God. When I came home, I looked to see if I could find that sentence in my heart—"Your righteousness is in heaven"—but could not find it. Therefore my heart began to sink again, but this verse was brought to my remembrance: "Of Him you are in Christ Jesus, who became for us wisdom from God—and righteousness and sanctification and redemption" (1 Corinthians 1:30).

231. For by this scripture I saw that the man Christ Jesus is our righteousness and sanctification before God, distinct from us regarding His bodily presence. Here, therefore, I lived for some time, very sweetly at peace with God through Christ. *Oh*, I thought, *Christ! Christ!* There was nothing but Christ before my eyes. I was not only interested in looking on this and the other benefits of Christ, including His blood, burial, and resurrection, but considered Him as a whole Christ!

232. It was glorious to me to see His exaltation and the worth and prevalence of all His benefits. Now Christ was all: all my wisdom, all my righteousness, all my sanctification, and all my redemption.

233. Further, the Lord also led me into the mystery of union with the Son of God, that I was joined to Him, that I was flesh of His flesh and bone of His bone, and now was Ephesians 5:30 a sweet word to me. By this also was my faith in Him as my righteousness the more confirmed to me; for if He and I were one, then His righteousness was mine, His merits mine, His victory mine. Now could I see myself in heaven and earth at once: in heaven by my Christ, my head, my righteousness and life, though on earth by my body or person.

234. Now I saw Christ Jesus was looked on by God—and should also be by us—as the person in whom the whole body of His elect is always to be considered and reckoned: that we fulfilled the law by Him, rose from the dead by Him, got the victory over sin, death, the devil, and hell by Him. When He died, we died, and so of His resurrection. " 'Your dead shall live; together with My dead body they shall arise,' " said he (Isaiah 26:19). Also, "After two days He will revive us; on the third day He will raise us up, that we may live in His sight" (Hosea 6:2). This is now fulfilled by the sitting down of the Son of Man on the right hand of the Majesty in the heavens, according to Ephesians 2:6: "[He] raised us up together, and made us sit together in the heavenly places in Christ Jesus." . . .

236. Having given you a taste of the sorrow and affliction that my soul went through because of the guilt and terror that my wicked thoughts put me under, and having also given you a touch of my deliverance from that guilt and the sweet comfort that I met with afterwards, which dwelt in my heart about a year, I will now, God willing, give you what, as I conceive, was the cause of this temptation, and also what advantage it became to my soul at last.

237. For the causes, I conceived they were principally two. The first was because I did not, when I was delivered from one temptation, pray to God to keep me from future temptations. For though my soul was much in prayer before this trial seized me, yet then I prayed mostly for the removal of present troubles and for fresh discoveries of His love in Christ. I saw afterwards this was not enough to do. I also should have prayed that God would keep me from the evil that was to come.

238. Of this I was made deeply aware by the prayer of David, who, when he was under present mercy, yet prayed that God would hold him back from future sin and temptation: "Then," said he, "I shall be blameless, and I shall be innocent of great transgression" (Psalm 19:13).

239. Hebrews 4:16 was another word that greatly condemned me for my folly in the neglect of this duty: "Let us therefore come boldly to the throne of grace, that we may obtain mercy and find grace to help in time of need." This I had not done, and therefore was allowed to sin and fall, according to what is written, "Pray that you enter not into temptation." And truly this very thing is to this day of such weight and awe upon me that I dare not, when I come before the Lord, get up off my knees until I entreat Him for help and mercy against the temptations that are to come. And I beseech you, reader, that you learn to beware of my negligence.

240. Another cause of this temptation was that I had tempted God, and in this manner did I do it: Once, my wife was great with child, and before her full time was come, her birth pangs were fierce and strong upon her, as if she had immediately fallen into labor and would deliver too early. Now, this was at the time that I was so strongly tempted to question the being of God; therefore, as my wife lay crying by me, I said, with all secrecy imaginable, even thinking in my heart, *Lord,* *if You will now remove this sad affliction from my wife and cause that she be troubled no more this night, then I will know that You can discern the most secret thoughts of the heart.*

241. I had no sooner said it in my heart than her pangs were taken from her and she fell into a deep sleep, and so she continued till morning. At this I greatly marveled, not knowing what to think, but after I had been awake a good while and heard her cry no more, I fell asleep also. So when I woke in the morning, what I had said in my heart the night before came to me again and how the Lord had showed me that He knew my secret thoughts, which was a great astonishment to me for several weeks.

242. Well, about a year and a half later, the sinful thought of which I have spoken before went through my wicked heart, even this thought: *Let Christ go if He will.* So when I was fallen under guilt for this, the remembrance of my other thought, and of the effect thereof, would come to me with this retort, which also carried rebuke with it: *Now you may see that God knows the most secret thoughts of the heart. . . .*

244. And now to show you something of the advantages that I also gained by this temptation. First, I was made to continually possess in my soul a wonderful sense of both the being and glory of God and of His beloved Son. In the temptation that went before, my soul was perplexed with unbelief; blasphemy; hardness of heart; questions about the being of God, Christ, the truth of the Word, and certainty of the world to come. I was greatly assaulted and tormented with atheism; but now the case was otherwise, now God and Christ were continually before my face, though not in a way of comfort but in a way of great dread and terror. The glory of the holiness of God at this time broke me to pieces, and the compassion of Christ broke me, for I could not consider Him but as a lost and rejected Christ.

245. The scriptures now also were wonderful to me; I saw that the truth of them was the key of the kingdom of heaven.

Those whom the scriptures favor must inherit bliss, but those whom they oppose and condemn must perish evermore. Oh! this word, "For the Scriptures cannot be broken," would rend my heart, and so would that other, " 'If you forgive the sins of any, they are forgiven them; if you retain the sins of any, they are retained' " (John 20:23). Now I saw the apostles to be the elders of the city of refuge (Joshua 20:4); those whom they were to receive were received to life, but those whom they shut out were to be slain by the avenger of blood. . . .

247. By this temptation I was made to see more into the nature of the promises than I ever was before, for I was now lying trembling under the mighty hand of God, continually torn by the thunderings of His justice. This made me, with careful heart and watchful eye and great seriousness, turn over every leaf and consider every sentence of scripture with much diligence.

248. By this temptation also I was greatly beaten off my former foolish practice of putting aside the word of promise when it came into my mind. For now, though I could not suck the comfort and sweetness from the promise as I had at other times, I would grab at all I saw. Before, I thought I might not meddle with the promise unless I felt its comfort, but now was not the time to do this; the avenger of blood too closely pursued me.

249. Now therefore I was glad to catch at that word that I still feared I had no right to own and even to leap into the bosom of that promise that I feared had shut its heart against me. Now also I would labor to take the Word as God had laid it down, without restraining the natural force of one syllable thereof. Oh, what did I now see in that sixth chapter of John: " 'The one who comes to Me I will by no means cast out' " (v. 37). Now I began to consider that God had a bigger mouth to speak with than I had heart to conceive with. I thought also that He spoke not His words in haste but with infinite wisdom and judgment, and in truth and faithfulness.

250. In those days, often in my greatest agonies, I would flounder toward the promise, concluding, though as one almost bereft of his wits because of fear, that on this I would rest and leave the fulfilling of it to the God of heaven who made it. Oh! many a pull has my heart had with Satan for that verse in the sixth chapter of John. I did not now, as at other times, look principally for comfort, though how welcome would it have been to me! But now a word, a word to lean a weary soul upon, that I might not sink forever! That was what I hunted for. . . .

252. I never saw those heights and depths of grace and love and mercy as I saw after this temptation. Great sins draw out great grace; and where guilt is most terrible and fierce, there the mercy of God in Christ appears most mighty when revealed to the soul. When Job had passed through his captivity, "the LORD gave [him] twice as much as he had before" (Job 42:10). Blessed be God for Jesus Christ our Lord.

Two or three times around the time of my deliverance from this temptation I had such strange apprehensions of the grace of God that I could hardly bear up under it, it was so amazing. I think that if that sense of it had dwelt long upon me, it would have made me incapable of business.

253. Now I shall relate other of the Lord's dealings with me at various other seasons and the temptations I then met. I will begin with what I encountered when I first joined the people of God in Bedford in fellowship. After I had propounded to the church that my desire was to walk in the ordinances of Christ with them and was admitted by them, the thought of Christ's last supper with His disciples before His death and the scripture " 'Do this in remembrance of Me' " (Luke 22:19) were made very precious to me. For by it the Lord came down on my conscience with the discovery of His death for my sins and made me feel as if He plunged me in the virtue of the same. But I had not been long a partaker of communion when fierce temptations attended me at all times to blaspheme it and to wish some deadly thing to happen to those who ate

thereof. I was forced to bend myself all
the while to pray to God to keep me from
such blasphemies and also to cry to God
to bless the bread and cup to them as it
went from mouth to mouth. The reason for
this temptation, I have thought since, was
because I did not at first approach to partake
thereof with the proper reverence.

254. I continued this way for three-quarters
of a year and never had rest or ease, but at
last the Lord came in upon my soul with
the same scripture by which my soul was
visited before. After that I was usually very
comfortable partaking of communion and
have, I trust, discerned the Lord's body as
broken for my sins and His precious blood
shed for my transgressions.

255. One spring when I was coming down
with a cold, I was suddenly and violently
seized with much physical weakness,
insomuch that I thought I could not
live. Now began I to give myself afresh
to a serious examination of my state and
condition for the future and of my evidences

for that blessed world to come; for it has, I bless the name of God, been my usual course to endeavor to keep my interest in the life to come clear before my eye.

256. But I had no sooner begun to recall to mind my former experience of the goodness of God to my soul than there came flocking into my mind an innumerable company of my sins and transgressions, among which these afflicted me most: my deadness, dullness, and coldness in holy duties; my wanderings of heart; my weariness in all good things; my lack of love for God, His ways, and people; and this at the end of all: *Are these the fruits of Christianity? Are these the tokens of a blessed man?*

257. At the apprehension of these things, my sickness was doubled upon me, for now was I sick in my inward man, my soul was clogged with guilt; now also was my former experience of God's goodness to me quite taken out of my mind and hidden as if it had never been. Now was my soul greatly pinched between these two considerations:

"Live I must not, die I dare not." Now my spirit sank, and I was giving up all for lost; but as I was walking up and down in the house in a most woeful state, this word of God took hold of my heart: "[You are] justified freely by His grace through the redemption that is in Christ Jesus" (Romans 3:24). But oh, what an effect it had on me!

258. Now was I as one awakened out of troubled sleep. It was as if I heard this heavenly sentence expounded to me: "Sinner, you think that because of your sins and infirmities I cannot save your soul, but behold, My Son is by Me, and upon Him I look and not on you and will deal with you according as I am pleased with Him." At this my mind was greatly lightened, and I was made to understand that God could justify a sinner at any time; it was but His looking upon Christ and imputing His benefits to us, and the work was done.

259. And as I was musing, this scripture also came with great power upon my spirit: "Not by works of righteousness which we have done, but according to His mercy He saved us" (Titus 3:5). Now was I raised on high; I saw myself within the arms of grace and mercy, and though I was afraid to think of the hour of my death before, now I cried, "Let me die!" Now death was lovely in my sight, for I saw we shall never live indeed till we are gone to the other world. Oh, I thought this life is but a slumber in comparison to that above; at this time also I saw more in those words, "heirs of God" (Romans 8:17), than ever I shall be able to express while I live in this world. Heirs of God! God Himself is the portion of the saints.

260. Another time when I was very ill and weak, the tempter assailed me strongly, for I find he is much for assaulting the soul when it begins to approach the grave. That is his opportunity to labor to hide from me my former experience of God's goodness, as well as set before me the terrors of death and the judgment of God. At this time, because of my fear of dying, I was as one dead before death came and felt as if I had already descended into the pit. But behold, just as I was in the midst of these fears, these words of the angels who carried Lazarus into Abraham's bosom darted in upon me: "So it shall be with you when you leave this world." This sweetly revived my spirit and helped me to hope in God. When I had with comfort mused on this awhile, this word fell with great weight upon my mind: "O Death, where is your sting? O Hades, where is your victory?" (1 Corinthians 15:55). At this I became well in both body and mind at once, and I walked comfortably in my work for God again.

261. At another time, though just before I was completely well and strong in my spirit, suddenly there fell upon me a great cloud of darkness that so hid from me the things of God that I felt as if I had never seen nor known them. My soul was also so overrun with a senseless, heartless frame of spirit that I could not feel my soul move or stir after grace and life by Christ. It was as if my loins were broken or as if my hands and feet had been tied or bound with chains. At this time also I felt some weakness seize upon my outward man, which made the other affliction the more heavy and uncomfortable to me.

262. After I had been in this condition three or four days, as I was sitting by the fire, I suddenly felt this word sound in my heart: "I must go to Jesus." At this my darkness and atheism fled and the blessed things of heaven were set within my view. Suddenly overtaken with surprise, I said, "Wife, is there a scripture that says, 'I must go to Jesus'?" She said she could not tell, therefore I sat musing to see if I could remember such a place. I had not sat more than two or three minutes than this came bolting in upon me: "To an innumerable company of angels" (Hebrews 12:22).

263. Then with joy I told my wife, "Oh, now I know, I know!" That night was a good night for me, I have had few better. I longed for the company of some of God's people that I might impart to them what God had shown me. Christ was a precious Christ to my soul that night; I could scarcely lie in my bed for joy and peace and triumph through Christ. This great glory did not continue upon me until morning, yet the passage in Hebrews was a blessed scripture to me for many days after this.

264. The full passage from Hebrews was this: "You have come to Mount Zion and to the city of the living God, the heavenly Jerusalem, to an innumerable company of angels, to the general assembly and church of the firstborn who are registered in heaven, to God the Judge of all, to the spirits of just men made perfect, to Jesus the Mediator of the new covenant, and to the blood of sprinkling that speaks better things than that of Abel" (Hebrews 12:22–24). Through this blessed sentence the Lord led me over and over, first to this word and then to that and showed me wonderful glory in every one of them. Since this time these words have often given great refreshment to my spirit. Blessed be God for having mercy on me.

A Brief Account of the Author's Call to the Work of the Ministry

265. Now I will throw in a word or two concerning my preaching of the Word and of God's dealing with me in that particular also. About five or six years after I had been awakened and helped to see the worth of Jesus Christ our Lord, and also enabled to venture my soul upon Him, some of the most able among the saints with us perceived that God had considered me worthy to understand something of His will in His holy and blessed Word and had given me ability, in some measure, to express to others what I saw for their edification. Therefore they desired earnestly that I would be willing to speak a word of exhortation at times to them at their meetings.

266. Though at first I was abashed, yet still being entreated by them, I consented to their request and shared my gift with them at two different assemblies, but in private and with much weakness and infirmity. At this they not only seemed to be both affected and comforted but solemnly protested that they were, and they gave thanks to the Father of mercies for the grace bestowed on me.

267. After this, sometimes when some of them went into the country to teach, they wanted me to go with them. Though I dared not make use of my gift in an open way, yet privately I came among the good people in those places and sometimes spoke a word of admonition to them. As the others had, they received the admonition with rejoicing at the mercy of God toward me, professing their souls were edified thereby.

268. Being still desired by the church and after some solemn prayer and fasting, I was more particularly called forth and appointed to a more public preaching of the Word, not only to and among those who believed but also to offer the Gospel to those who had not yet received the faith. About this time I found in my mind a secret desire to move

forward in that calling, though, I bless God,
not for my own glory, for at that time I was
most sorely afflicted with the fiery darts of
the devil concerning my eternal state.

269. Yet I could not be content unless I
was found in the exercise of my gift, to
which I was greatly animated not only by
the continual desires of the godly but also
by this saying of Paul to the Corinthians:
"I urge you, brethren—you know the
household of Stephanas, that it is the
firstfruits of Achaia, and that they have
devoted themselves to the ministry of the
saints—that you also submit to such, and to
everyone who works and labors with us" (1
Corinthians 16:15–16).

270. By this text I was made to see that
the Holy Spirit never intended that men
who have gifts and abilities should bury
them but rather commanded and stirred
up such to the exercise of their gift and
also commended those who were ready to
do so. "They have devoted themselves to
the ministry of the saints" (1 Corinthians

16:15). This scripture continually ran through my mind, to encourage me and strengthen me in this work for God. I was also encouraged by several other scriptures and examples of the godly, both in the Word and other ancient histories.

271. Therefore, though I myself am the most unworthy of all the saints, I set about the work, though with great fear and trembling, and preached the blessed Gospel that God had shown me in the holy Word of truth, according to my gift and the proportion of my faith. When people in the country understood, they came in by the hundreds to hear the Word.

272. And I thank God He gave me some measure of compassion for their souls, which spurred me to labor with great diligence and earnestness to find words that might, if God would bless them, awaken the conscience. For I had not preached long before some began to be touched by the Word and to be greatly afflicted in their minds at the awareness of the greatness of their sin and of their need for Jesus Christ.

273. But at first I could not believe that
God would speak through me to the heart of
any man, still considering myself unworthy,
yet those who were touched loved me and
had respect for me. And though I denied
that they could be awakened by me, still
they would confess it and affirm it before the
saints of God. They also blessed God for me,
unworthy wretch that I am! and counted me
God's instrument that showed them the way
of salvation.

274. Therefore, seeing them in both their
words and deeds to be so constant, and also
in their hearts to be earnestly pressing after
the knowledge of Jesus Christ, rejoicing that
God had sent me to them, then I began to
conclude it might be that God had owned
in His work such a foolish one as I. Then
came this word of God to my heart with
much sweet refreshment: "The blessing of a
perishing man came upon me, and I caused
the widow's heart to sing for joy" (Job 29:13).

275. At this, therefore, I rejoiced. Indeed, the tears of those whom God awakened by my preaching would be both solace and encouragement to me, for I thought on these sayings: "Who is he who makes me glad but the one who is made sorrowful by me?" (2 Corinthians 2:2); and also, "If I am not an apostle to others, yet doubtless I am to you. For you are the seal of my apostleship in the Lord" (1 Corinthians 9:2). These things, therefore, were as another argument to me that God had called me to this work and stood by me in it.

276. In my preaching of the Word, I took special notice of this one thing: namely, that the Lord led me to begin where His Word begins with sinners, that is, to condemn all flesh and to allege that the curse of God, by the law, belongs to and lays hold on all men as they come into the world because of sin. Now this part of my work I fulfilled with great sense, for the terrors of the law and guilt for my transgressions lay heavy on my conscience. I preached what I felt, even that which my poor soul groaned and trembled under.

277. Indeed I have been as one sent to
them from the dead; I went myself in chains
to preach to those who were in chains and
carried the fire in my own conscience that
I persuaded them to beware of. I can truly
say that when I have been on my way to
preach, I have been full of guilt and terror
even to the pulpit door, and there it has
been removed and I have been at liberty in
my mind until I have done my work. Then
immediately, even before I could get down
the pulpit stairs, I have been as bad as I was
before; yet God carried me on with a strong
hand, for neither guilt nor hell could keep
me from my work.

278. Thus I went for the space of two years,
crying out against men's sins and their fearful
state because of them. After this the Lord
came in upon my own soul with some peace
and comfort through Christ, for He gave
me many sweet discoveries of His blessed
grace through Him. So now I altered my
preaching. I still preached what I saw and
felt; now I labored much to hold forth
Jesus Christ in all His offices and benefits

to the world and strove also to discover, to condemn, and to remove those false supports and props on which the world leans, and by them falls and perishes. On these things also I stayed as long as on the other.

279. After this, God led me into something of the mystery of union with Christ, which I showed to them also. And when I had traveled through these three chief points of the Word of God for about five years or more, I was caught in my present practice and cast into prison, where I have lain as long again, to confirm the truth by way of suffering, as I was before in testifying of it according to the scriptures by way of preaching.

280. When I have been preaching, I thank God, my heart has often cried to God that He would make the Word effective in bringing salvation to the soul, still being concerned that the enemy might take the Word away from the conscience and become unfruitful. Therefore I labored to speak the Word in such a way that if it were possible,

the person guilty of that particular sin might
be convicted of it.

281. Also, when I have been preaching, it
has concerned me deeply to think that the
Word might fall as rain on stony places. I
wished from my heart, *Oh, that those who
have heard me speak this day could but see
as I do what sin, death, hell, and the curse of
God are; and also what the grace, love, and
mercy of God are, through Christ, to men in
such a case as they are, who are yet estranged
from Him.* And, indeed, I often said in my
heart before the Lord, *If being hanged before
their eyes would be a means to awaken them
and confirm them in the truth, I would be
contented.*

282. For I have often felt in my preaching,
especially when I have been engaged in the
doctrine of life in Christ, as if an angel of
God stood at my back to encourage me. Oh,
that doctrine has filled my own soul with
such power and heavenly evidence while I
have been laboring to unfold it, demonstrate
it, and fasten it upon the consciences of

others that I could not be content with just saying, "I believe and am sure." I thought I was more than sure, if it be lawful to express myself that way, that the things I asserted were true.

283. When I first began to preach the Word in neighboring towns, the doctors and priests of the country protested loudly against me. But I was persuaded not to repay railing for railing but to see how many carnal believers I could convince of their miserable state according to the law, as well as the worth of Christ. For, thought I, "So my righteousness will answer for me in time to come, when the subject of my wages comes before you" (Genesis 30:33).

284. I never cared to meddle with arguments and disputes among the saints, especially things of the lowest nature; yet it pleased me much to contend with great earnestness for the Word of faith and the remission of sins by the death and sufferings of Jesus. But as for other things, I left them alone, because I saw they engendered strife

and because they do not commend us to
God or show that we are His. Besides, I saw
my work before me ran in another channel:
to carry an awakening word. To that work
therefore did I adhere. . . .

286. If any of those who were awakened
by my ministry fell back, as sometimes too
many did, I can truly say their loss affected
me more than if one of my own children
had been dying. I think I may say without
offence to the Lord that nothing has so
affected me as that, unless it was the fear of
the loss of the salvation of my own soul. I
have considered that I had good buildings
and lordships in those places where my
children were born; my heart has been so
wrapped up in the glory of this excellent
work that I counted myself more blessed
and honored of God than if He had made
me the emperor of the Christian world or
the lord of all the glory of the earth! Oh,
these words: "He who turns a sinner from the
error of his way will save a soul from death
and cover a multitude of sins" (James 5:20).
"The fruit of the righteous is a tree of life,

and he who wins souls is wise" (Proverbs 11:30). "Those who are wise shall shine like the brightness of the firmament, and those who turn many to righteousness like the stars forever and ever" (Daniel 12:3). "For what is our hope, or joy, or crown of rejoicing? Is it not even you in the presence of our Lord Jesus Christ at His coming? For you are our glory and joy" (1 Thessalonians 2:19–20). These, with many others of a like nature, have been great refreshments to me.

287. I have observed that where I have had a work to do for God, I have had first the desire to preach there. I have also observed that certain souls in particular have been strongly put on my heart, and I have been stirred up to pray for their salvation. As a result, these very souls have been drawn in as the fruits of my ministry. I have also observed that a word cast in incidentally has done more good in a sermon than all that was spoken besides. Sometimes also when I have thought I did not do any good, then I did the most of all; and at other times when I thought I would catch them I have fished for nothing.

288. I have also observed that where there
has been a work to do upon sinners, there
the devil has begun to roar in the hearts and
by the mouths of his servants. Indeed, often
when the wicked world has raged most,
souls have been awaked by the Word.

289. My great desire in fulfilling my
ministry was to get into the darkest places of
the country, even among those people who
were furthest from professing salvation. Yet
not because I could not endure the light,
for I feared not to show my Gospel to any,
but because I found my spirit leaned most
toward awakening and converting work, and
the Word that I carried led most that way
also. Indeed, so have I strived to preach the
Gospel where Christ was not named, "lest I
should build on another man's foundation"
(Romans 15:20).

290. In my preaching I have really been in
pain and have, as it were, labored to bring
forth children to God, neither could I be
satisfied unless some fruits appeared in my
work. If I were fruitless it mattered not who

commended me; but if I were fruitful, I cared not who condemned. I have thought of that verse, "He who wins souls is wise" (Proverbs 11:30); and another, "Behold, children are a heritage from the LORD, the fruit of the womb is a reward. Like arrows in the hand of a warrior, so are the children of one's youth. Happy is the man who has his quiver full of them; they shall not be ashamed, but shall speak with their enemies in the gate" (Psalm 127:3–5).

291. It did not please me at all to see people drink in opinions if they seemed ignorant of Jesus Christ and the worth of their own salvation. Sound conviction for sin, especially for unbelief, and a heart set on fire to be saved by Christ, with strong desire for a truly sanctified soul, that was what delighted me; those were the souls I counted blessed.

292. But in this work, as in all others, temptations of various kinds attended me, as sometimes I would be assaulted with great discouragement about it, fearing that I would not be able to speak the Word at all

to edification or be able to speak sense to
the people. At times like this such a strange
faintness and weakness would seize my body
that my legs would scarcely be able to carry
me to the place of preaching.

293. Sometimes also when I have been
preaching, I have been violently assaulted
with thoughts of blasphemy and strongly
tempted to speak the words before the
congregation. Sometimes, even when I have
begun by speaking the Word with much
clarity and liberty of speech, before the end
of my sermon I have been so disoriented and
estranged from the things I was speaking
about, as well as unable to utter the words
clearly, that I have felt as if I did not know
or remember what I was talking about, or as
if my head were in a bag.

294. Sometimes when I have been about
to preach on some scorching portion of the
Word, I have found the tempter suggest,
"What, will you preach this? This condemns
yourself; of this your own soul is guilty.
Therefore do not preach on it at all, or if

you do, yet so mince your words as to make a way for your own escape, lest instead of awakening others, you lay that guilt upon your own soul that you will never be able to get out from under."

295. But, I thank the Lord, I have been kept from consenting to these horrid suggestions and have, as Samson, bowed myself with all my might to condemn sin and transgression wherever I found it, even though therein also I brought guilt upon my own conscience! *Let me die*, thought I, *with the Philistines* (Judges 16:29–30), *rather than deal corruptly with the blessed Word of God.* "You, therefore, who teach another, do you not teach yourself?" (Romans 2:21). It is far better that you do judge yourself, even by preaching plainly to others, than that you imprison the truth in unrighteousness to save yourself. Blessed be God for His help also in this.

296. I have also, while in this blessed work of Christ, been often tempted to harbor pride of heart; and though I dare not say I have not been infected with it, yet I have had but small joy in giving way to it. For it has been my portion every day to be let into the evil of my own heart and made to see such a multitude of corruptions and infirmities that it has made me hang down my head under all my gifts and attainments. I have felt this thorn in the flesh, the very mercy of God to me (2 Corinthians 12:7–9).

297. I have also had some notable passages of the Word presented to me that contained some sharp and piercing sentences concerning the perishing of the soul, in spite of gifts and abilities. This verse, for instance, has been of great use to me: "Though I speak with the tongues of men and of angels, but have not love, I have become sounding brass or a clanging cymbal" (1 Corinthians 13:1).

298. A tinkling cymbal is an instrument of music with which a skillful player can make such melodious and heart-inflaming music that all who hear him play can scarcely keep from dancing. And yet the cymbal has no life, neither does the music come from it, but it is the result of the skill of him who plays it. So then the instrument at last may come to nothing and perish, though in the past such music has been made on it.

299. I saw how it was and will be with those who have gifts but lack saving grace. They are in the hand of Christ like the cymbal in the hand of David; and as David could make mirth in the service of God with the cymbal to elevate the hearts of the worshippers, so Christ can use gifted men to affect the souls of His people in His church. Yet when He has done all, He can hang them up as lifeless, though sounding, cymbals.

300. This consideration, therefore, together with some others, was, for the most part, as a hammer on the head of pride. *What?* thought I, *shall I be proud because I am a sounding brass? Is it so much to be a fiddle? Does not the least creature that has life have more of God in it than these?* Besides, I knew it is love that never dies, but other things must cease and vanish. So I concluded that a little grace, a little love, a little of

the true fear of God is better than all these
gifts. Indeed, I am fully convinced that
it is possible for a soul that can scarcely
give a man an answer to have a thousand
times more grace and so to be more in the
love and favor of the Lord than some who
have the gift of knowledge and can deliver
themselves like angels. . . .

302. This showed me, too, that gifts by
themselves are dangerous, not in themselves,
but because of those evils that attend those
who have them, that is, pride, vanity, self-
conceit, etc., all of which expand at the
applause of every unadvised Christian,
putting the poor creature in danger of falling
under the condemnation of the devil.

303. I saw, therefore, that he who has gifts
needs to see that they come short of putting
him in a truly saved condition, lest he rest in
them and so fall short of the grace of God.

304. He also has cause to walk humbly
with God and be small in his own eyes and
remember that his gifts are not his own, but

the church's, and that by them he is made
a servant to the church and must give at
last an account of his stewardship to the
Lord Jesus. And to give a good account is a
blessed thing.

305. Let all men therefore prize a little the
fear of the Lord. Gifts indeed are desirable,
yet great grace and small gifts are better than
great gifts and no grace. Scripture does not
say "the Lord gives gifts and glory" but "the
Lord gives grace and glory." And blessed is
the one to whom the Lord gives grace, true
grace, for that is a certain forerunner of
glory.

306. But when Satan perceived that
tempting and assaulting me this way would
not achieve his design to overthrow my
ministry and make it ineffective, he tried
another way, which was to stir up the minds
of the ignorant and malicious to cover me
with slanders and reproaches. Now I may
say that what the devil could devise and his
instruments invent was broadcast up and
down the countryside against me, thinking,

as I said, that by that means they could
make me abandon my ministry.

307. It began, therefore, to be rumored
among the people that I was a witch, a
Jesuit, a highwayman, and the like.

308. To all of these rumors I will only say,
God knows that I am innocent. But as for
my accusers, let them prepare themselves
to meet me before the tribunal of the Son
of God, where they will answer for these
things, along with the rest of their iniquities,
unless God grants them repentance, for
which I pray with all my heart.

309. But that which was reported with the
boldest confidence was that I had mistresses,
visited whores, sired bastards, indeed, that I
had two wives at the same time, and the like.
Now these slanders, along with the others,
I glory in, because they are but slanders,
foolish lies, and falsehoods cast on me by the
devil and his seed, and if I am not dealt with
wickedly by the world, I would lack one
sign of a saint and a child of God. " 'Blessed

are you,' " said the Lord Jesus, " 'when they revile and persecute you, and say all kinds of evil against you falsely for My sake. Rejoice and be exceedingly glad, for great is your reward in heaven, for so they persecuted the prophets who were before you' " (Matthew 5:11–12).

310. For my own sake, therefore, these things do not trouble me. I have a good conscience, and whereas they speak evil of me, those who falsely accuse my good conduct in Christ will be ashamed.

311. So then, what shall I say to those who have thus besmirched my name? Shall I threaten them? Shall I chide them? Shall I flatter them? Shall I entreat them to hold their tongues? No, not I. Were it not for the fact that these things make them ripe for damnation, I would say to them, "Report it, because it will increase my glory."

312. Therefore I bind these lies and slanders to me as an ornament. It belongs to my Christian profession to be vilified, slandered,

reproached, and reviled. As my God and
my conscience bear me witness, I rejoice in
reproaches for Christ's sake. . . .

314. My foes have missed their mark in
their shooting at me. I am not the man. I
wish that they themselves were guiltless. If
all the fornicators and adulterers in England
were hanged by the neck till they were dead,
John Bunyan would be still alive and well.

315. And in this I admire the wisdom of
God, that He made me shy around women
from my conversion until now. Those who
know me best know that it is a rare thing
to see me carry on a conversation with a
woman.

316. And now to wind up this matter, I am
calling not only men but angels to prove
me guilty of having done anything carnally
with any woman but my wife. And knowing
that I cannot offend the Lord in such a case,
I am calling on God for a record upon my
soul that in these things I am innocent.
Not that I have been thus kept because of

any goodness in me more than any other, but God has been merciful to me and has kept me, to whom I pray that He will keep me still, not only from this but from every evil way and work, and preserve me to His heavenly kingdom. Amen.

317. Now as Satan labored by reproaches and slanders to make me vile among my countrymen, that, if possible, my preaching might be made of no effect, so there was added a long and tedious imprisonment that thereby I might be frightened from my service for Christ and the world made afraid to hear me preach, of which I shall, in the next section, give you a brief account.

A Brief Account of the Author's Imprisonment

318. Having made profession of the glorious Gospel of Christ for a long time and preached it for about five years, I was apprehended at a meeting of good people in the country, among whom I was supposed to preach that day. But they took me away and brought me before a justice, who imprisoned me, even after I offered security for my appearance at the next sessions, because I would not consent to be bound that I should no longer preach to the people.

319. At the sessions, after I was indicted for being an upholder and maintainer of unlawful assemblies and secret meetings and for not conforming to the national worship of the Church of England, the justices sentenced me to perpetual banishment, because I refused to conform. So, being again delivered up to a jailer's hands, I was taken to prison and there have lain now for twelve years, waiting to see what God would allow those men to do with me.

320. In this condition I have continued with much contentment, through grace, but have experienced much tumult in my heart, because of the Lord, Satan, and my own corruption. For all, glory be to Jesus Christ! I have also received much conviction, instruction, and understanding, which I will not discuss here in detail, only to give you a hint or two, a word that may stir up the godly to bless God and to pray for me, and also to give encouragement to not fear what man can do to them, should they ever be in such a case.

321. I have never in all my life had so great an inlet into the Word of God as now. The scriptures that I saw nothing in before are made to shine on me in this place and state. Jesus Christ also has never been more real and apparent than now; here I have seen and felt Him indeed. Oh! that word, "We did not follow cunningly devised fables" (2 Peter 1:16), and, "God. . .raised Him from the dead and gave Him glory, so that your faith and hope are in God" (1 Peter 1:21) were blessed words to me in my imprisoned condition.

322. These scriptures also have been great refreshments to me: John 14:1–4; John 16:33; Colossians 3:3–4; Hebrews 12:22–24. Sometimes when I have been savoring them I have been able to laugh at destruction and to fear neither the horse nor his rider. I have had sweet sights of the forgiveness of my sins in this place and of my being with Jesus in another world. Oh! Mount Zion, the heavenly Jerusalem, the innumerable company of angels, and God the judge of all, and the spirits of just men made perfect, and Jesus (Hebrews 12:22–24) have been sweet to me in this place. I have seen a truth in this scripture that I am persuaded I will never be able to express in this world: "Whom having not seen you love. Though now you do not see Him, yet believing, you rejoice with joy inexpressible and full of glory" (1 Peter 1:8).

323. I never knew what it was like to have God stand by me at every turn and every offer of Satan to afflict me as I have found Him since I came here. For as fears have presented themselves, so have support and encouragement. Indeed, when I have startled at nothing more than my shadow, God, being very tender toward me, has not allowed me to be molested, but has, with one scripture or another, strengthened me against every fear, to the extent that I have often said, "If it were lawful, I would pray for greater trouble, in order that I might enjoy greater comfort." (See Ecclesiastes 7:14; 2 Corinthians 1:5.)

324. Before I came to prison I saw what was coming and had two considerations warm upon my heart: first, how to encounter death, if that were my portion. For the first of these, Colossians 1:11 was great encouragement to me, namely, to pray to God to be "strengthened with all might, according to His glorious power, for all patience and longsuffering with joy." This sentence or sweet petition would, as it were, thrust itself into my mind and persuade me that, if I were ever to go through suffering, I must have patience, especially if I wanted to endure it joyfully.

325. As for the second consideration, this saying was of great use to me: "Yes, we had the sentence of death in ourselves, that we should not trust in ourselves but in God who raises the dead" (2 Corinthians 1:9). By this scripture I was made to see that if I was to ever suffer rightly, I must first pass a sentence of death upon everything that can properly be called a thing of this life, even to reckon myself, my wife, my children, my health, my enjoyments, and all as dead to me, and myself as dead to them.

326. The second was to live for God, who is invisible, as Paul said in another place: the way not to faint is to "not look at the things which are seen, but at the things which are not seen. For the things which are seen are temporary, but the things which are not seen are eternal" (2 Corinthians 4:18). And thus I reasoned with myself, *If I prepare only for a prison, then the whip comes without warning, and so also does the pillory. Again, if I only prepare for these, then I am not fit for banishment. Furthermore, if I conclude that banishment is the worst, then if death comes*

I am surprised. So the way I see it, the best way to go through suffering is to trust in God through Christ concerning the world to come, and concerning this world, to consider the grave my house, to make my bed in darkness, to "say to corruption, 'You are my father,' and to the worm, 'You are my mother and my sister,'" (Job 17:14); that is, to become familiar with these things.

327. But in spite of these helps, I found myself a man encompassed by infirmities. Parting with my wife and poor children has often been to me in this place as the pulling of the flesh from the bones, not only because I am somewhat too fond of these great mercies, but also because I often thought of the many hardships, miseries, and wants my poor family was likely to encounter if I should be taken from them, especially my poor blind child, who was nearer my heart than all the others. Oh! the thoughts of the hardship I thought my poor blind one might experience broke my heart to pieces.

328. *Poor child!* thought I. *What sorrow are you likely to have for your portion in this world! You must be beaten, must beg, suffer hunger, cold, nakedness, and a thousand calamities, though I cannot now endure that the wind should blow on you.* Yet recalling myself, I thought, *I must trust you all to God, though it cuts to the quick to leave you.* Oh! I saw in this condition I was as a man who was pulling down his house upon the head of his wife and children. *Yet*, thought I, *I must do it, I must do it.*

329. But what helped me in this temptation was various considerations, three of which I will name here: The first was the consideration of these two scriptures: "Leave your fatherless children, I will preserve them alive; and let your widows trust in Me" (Jeremiah 49:11); and "The Lord said, 'Surely it will be well with your remnant; surely I will cause the enemy to intercede with you in the time of adversity and in the time of affliction' " (Jeremiah 15:11).

330. I also had this consideration, that if I ventured all for God, I engaged God to take care of my concerns. But if I forsook Him in His ways, for fear of any trouble that might come to me or mine, then I would not only falsify my profession but would make it appear that my concerns were not as well cared for if left at God's feet while I stood for His name, as they would be if they were under my own care but with my denial of the way of God. This was a painful consideration. Another scripture that greatly helped fasten this consideration on me was where Christ prayed against Judas that God would disappoint him in his selfish thoughts that moved him to sell his master. I urge you to read it soberly: Psalm 109:6–20.

331. I had also another consideration and that was the dread of the torments of hell, of which I was sure those who, for fear of the cross, shrink from their profession of Christ and His words and laws before the sons of men must partake. I thought also of the glory that He had prepared for those who in faith, love, and patience stood for His ways.

These things have helped me when thoughts have plagued my mind of the misery that both myself and mine might be exposed to, because of my profession.

332. When I indeed recognized that I might be banished for my profession, I thought of this scripture: "They were stoned, they were sawn in two, were tempted, were slain with the sword. They wandered about in sheepskins and goatskins, being destitute, afflicted, tormented—as of whom the world was not worthy" (Hebrews 11:37–38). I also thought of this saying: "The Holy Spirit testifies in every city, saying that chains and tribulations await me" (Acts 20:23).

333. I was once in a very sad and low condition for many weeks, at which time I, being a young prisoner and not acquainted with the laws, had this weighing on my spirits: that my imprisonment might end at the gallows for all that I could tell. Now therefore Satan laid hard at me, to discourage me by suggesting this to me: "But what if, when you come to die, you should be in this condition, that is, not savoring the things of God nor having any evidence upon your soul for a better state hereafter?" For indeed at this time all the things of God were hidden from my soul.

334. When I first began to think of this, it was a great trouble to me, for I thought that I was not fit to die in the condition I was now in; neither, indeed, did I think I could if I were called to it. Besides, I thought, if I climbed up the ladder to my execution with quaking or other symptoms of fainting, I would give the enemy cause to reproach the way of God and His people for their timorousness. This, therefore, greatly troubled me, for I thought I was ashamed to die with a pale face and tottering knees in such a way.

335. Therefore I prayed to God that He would comfort me and give me strength to do and suffer what He would call me to. Yet no comfort appeared but all continued hidden. I was also at this time so possessed with the thought of death that often I felt as if I were on the ladder with a rope about my neck. Only this was some encouragement to me: I thought I might now have an opportunity to speak my last words to a multitude, which I thought would come to see me die. And I thought, if it must be so, if God will convert just one soul by my last words, I will not count my life thrown away nor lost.

336. Yet all the things of God were kept out of my sight, and still the tempter followed me with "But where will you go when you die? What will become of you? Where will you be found in another world? What evidence have you for heaven and glory and an inheritance among those who are sanctified?" Thus was I tossed for many weeks and knew not what to do. At last this consideration fell with weight on me: that it was for the Word and way of God that I was in this condition. Therefore I was encouraged not to flinch a hair's breadth from it.

337. I thought also that God could choose whether He would give me comfort now or at the hour of death, but I might not therefore choose whether I would hold to my profession of faith or not. I was bound, but He was free; indeed, it was my duty to stand on His Word, whether He would ever look on me or save me at the last. *Therefore,* thought I, *I am for going on and venturing my eternal state with Christ, whether I have comfort here or not. If God does not come in,* thought I, *I will leap off the ladder into eternity, even blindfolded, sink or swim, come heaven, come hell. Lord Jesus, if You will catch me, do; if not, I will venture for Your name.*

338. I was no sooner fixed with this resolution than this word came to me: " 'Does Job fear God for nothing?' " (Job 1:9). It was as if the accuser had said, "Lord, Job is no upright man. Does he serve You for nothing? Have You not made a hedge about him? But put forth now Your hand and touch all that he has, and he will curse You to Your face." *How now,* thought I, *is this the sign of an upright soul, to desire to*

*serve God when all is taken from him? Is there
a godly man that will serve God for nothing
rather than give out?* Blessed be God, then
I hope I have an upright heart, for I am
resolved, God giving me strength, to never
deny my profession of faith, though I gained
nothing at all for my pains. And as I was
thus considering, this scripture was laid on
my heart: Psalm 44:12–26.

339. Now was my heart full of comfort,
for I hoped it was sincere. I would not
have been without this trial for much. I
am comforted every time I think of it,
and I hope I will bless God forever for the
teaching I have gained from it. Many more
of the dealings of God toward me I might
relate, but these, out of the spoils won in
battles, have I dedicated to maintain the
house of God (1 Chronicles 26:27).

CONCLUSION

1. Of all the temptations that I have met with in my life, to question the being of God and the truth of His Gospel is the worst, and the worst to be borne. When this temptation comes, it takes away the belt of truth from me and removes the foundations from under me. Oh, I have often thought of that word, "Having girded your waist with truth" (Ephesians 6:14), and, "If the foundations are destroyed, what can the righteous do?" (Psalm 11:3).

2. Sometimes, after committing sin, I have expected sore chastisement from the hand of God, only to receive from Him a discovery of His grace. Sometimes, when I have been comforted, I have called myself a fool for sinking under trouble. And then, again, when I have been cast down, I have thought I was not wise to give way to comfort. With such strength and weight have both of these been upon me.

3. I have wondered much at this one thing: that though God visits my soul with a blessed discovery of Himself, I have found that afterward my spirit has been so filled with darkness that I could not conceive what that comfort was with which I was refreshed.

4. I have sometimes seen more in a line of the Bible than I could very well tell how to stand under, and yet at other times the whole Bible has been as dry as a stick, or rather, my heart has been so dry and dead to it that I could not conceive the least drop of refreshment, though I have looked all over for it.

5. Of all tears, the best ones are those that are made by the blood of Christ; and of all joy, the sweetest is that which is mixed with mourning over Christ. Oh! it is a good thing to be on our knees, with Christ in our arms, before God. I hope I know something of these things.

6. I find to this day seven abominations in my heart: (1) an inclination to unbelief;

(2) suddenly forgetting the love and mercy that Christ manifests; (3) a leaning toward the works of the law; (4) wanderings and coldness in prayer; (5) forgetting to watch what I pray for; (6) being apt to murmur because I have no more and yet ready to abuse what I have; (7) I can do none of those things that God commands me, but my corruptions will thrust themselves forward. "When I would do good, evil is present with me" (Romans 7:21 KJV).

7. These things I continually see and feel and am afflicted and oppressed with, yet the wisdom of God orders them for my good: (1) They make me abhor myself; (2) They keep me from trusting my heart; (3) They convince me of the insufficiency of all inherent righteousness; (4) They show me the necessity of fleeing to Jesus; (5) They press me to pray to God; (6) They show me the need I have to watch and be sober; (7) And they provoke me to look to God, through Christ, to help me and carry me through this world. Amen.

Look for All of the FAITH CLASSICS from Barbour Publishing

Barbour's Faith Classics offer compelling, updated text and an easy-reading typesetting, all in a fresh new trim size. Introduce a new generation to these books worth reading!

Confessions
by Saint
Augustine

The God of All
Comfort
by Hannah
Whitall Smith

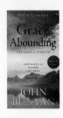

Grace
Abounding
by John Bunyan

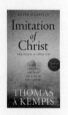

The Imitation
of Christ
by Thomas à
Kempis

In the
Twinkling of
an Eye
by Sydney
Watson

Quiet Talks
on Prayer
by S.D. Gordon

Each title: Paperback / 4.1875" x 7.5" / 192 pages

Available wherever Christian books are sold.